What people are saying about …

GOD CAN'T SLEEP

"In a world full of pain, Palmer's global stories of hope engaged and inspired me to see a God who shows up and knows my name."

Chris Clark, founder and president of
Children of the Nations, www.cotni.org

"In *God Can't Sleep* Palmer tells both beautiful and heartbreaking stories. He is not scared to stare suffering in the face, embrace paradox, and ask hard questions. I'm grateful for his honesty and refreshing insight into the relentless love of God."

Jack Mooring, singer, songwriter, and
keyboardist for the band Leeland

Praise for …

"*True Religion* will ⎯⎯⎯⎯⎯⎯⎯ our soul. If your heart and soul have been cold to the trouble in this world, then you must read this book. Palmer Chinchen challenges armchair quarterbacks everywhere to get off the couch and give their lives away to change what is broken in this world."

Kurt Warner, NFL quarterback
and two-time league MVP

"What medicine would you prescribe for what ails the church? I'd suggest a strong dose of what Palmer Chinchen serves up in this book. Reading *True Religion* will transform lives—and entire congregations. This book should be required reading for twenty-first- century Christians."

Duane Litfin, president of Wheaton College

"We all owe a debt of gratitude to Palmer for taking us beyond the stagnation of self-absorbed spirituality to the joy of pouring our lives out to others in radical ways. If you're wondering what's missing in life, *True Religion* just may be your answer!"

Joseph Stowell, president of
Cornerstone University

"Warning: This book will disturb you. It also may change your life and your lifestyle for the better. Palmer Chinchen comes from a family who did give up their lives and change their lifestyles for the sake of others because of the gospel. This focus on others saturates Palmer's book. May it come to saturate your life and mine as well."

Dr. Robert (Ric) C. Cannada Jr., chancellor
and CEO of Reformed Theological Seminary

"*True Religion* reminds me that to be Christlike means to be bothered by injustice. Palmer's true stories soften my heart toward the lost and the hurting and make me excited to give generously, just as Christ gives generously to me."

JJ Heller, singer and songwriter

"Chinchen teaches us to open our eyes to the brokenness of the world and practice true religion, as Jesus defined it, which is to love first and love much. With many ideas for how to become the 'expatriate'—and take God's mercy to places beyond our comfort zone—this book stretches believers to not only see Christ in every human need but to actually do something about it."

Dr. Barry H. Corey, president of Biola University

GOD CAN'T SLEEP

Waiting for Daylight on Life's Dark Nights

Palmer Chinchen, PhD

David C Cook®
transforming lives together

GOD CAN'T SLEEP
Published by David C Cook
4050 Lee Vance View
Colorado Springs, CO 80918 U.S.A.

David C Cook Distribution Canada
55 Woodslee Avenue, Paris, Ontario, Canada N3L 3E5

David C Cook U.K., Kingsway Communications
Eastbourne, East Sussex BN23 6NT, England

David C Cook and the graphic circle C logo
are registered trademarks of Cook Communications Ministries.

Some names have been changed throughout for privacy purposes.

The website addresses recommended throughout this book are offered as a
resource to you. These websites are not intended in any way to be or imply an
endorsement on the part of David C Cook, nor do we vouch for their content.

Bible translation references can be found on page 235.

LCCN 2011923886
ISBN 978-1-4347-0057-5
eISBN 978-1-4347-0400-9

Published in association with the literary agency of Creative Trust,
Inc., 5141 Virginia Way, Suite 320, Brentwood, TN 37027

The Team: Don Pape, John Blase, Amy Kiechlin,
Sarah Schultz, Caitlyn York, Karen Athen
Cover Design: Rule 29
Back Cover Photo: Josh Hailey
Interior Images: Scott Erickson

Printed in the United States of America

First Edition 2011

1 2 3 4 5 6 7 8 9 10

032911

This book is dedicated to the people of
Haiti.
Your pain is deeper than I will ever know,
Je suis très désolé.
Our God has not forgotten you,
neither will we.

ACKNOWLEDGMENTS

Deepest gratitude to each of you who made this book possible:

Kathy Helmers: I am incredibly privileged to work with one of the finest literary minds of our day. Without you as my literary agent, this book would still be just another Word document.

Jim Chaffee: The English language is short on words that sufficiently express my gratitude.

Don Pape: You inspire me.

Ginia Hairston: Thank you for believing in the message of my books.

Terry Behimer, Marilyn Largent, Jeremy Potter, John Blase, Caitlyn York, and everyone else at David C Cook: Thank you for sharing your beautiful talents with me.

Dan Raines, Meredith Smith, and all at Creative Trust: Thank you!

Kelly Hughes: So good to partner with you.

The Grove: I could never do it without you.

Veronica: You make our life together a beautiful adventure.

Byron, Spencer, Christian, and William: You make your dad proud every day.

CONTENTS

FOREWORD

By Matt Hammitt
Grammy nominated singer, songwriter,
and lead singer of Sanctus Real

In the fourteen years that I've been touring with Sanctus Real, I've visited over a thousand cities in America and other parts of the world. I've wandered through neighborhoods and suburbs and have stood in the shadows of skyscrapers and cathedrals. At the center of every city is a competition for glory, where men and women devote their lives to building monuments for the sake of their own greatness and pleasure. These earthly kingdoms appeal to our human senses, offering us the greatest of attractions and the most beautiful distractions. Whether you're walking the strip in Vegas, buying a ticket to the movies, or gazing at beautiful people on the streets and on magazine covers, a taste of worldly glory is available at every corner.

In Matthew, at the end of a forty-day fast, "the devil took [Jesus] to a very high mountain and showed Him all the kingdoms of the world and their glory; and he said to Him, 'All these things I will give

You, if You fall down and worship me.'"[1] This is the first time in the New Testament that we see Jesus suffer temptation. He was hungry and weak, probably longing for physical gratification. Still, it doesn't seem that brilliant of the Devil to tempt the Creator of heaven and earth with worldly pleasures. I'm left to wonder if the Father permitted the Devil to tempt Jesus in this way for *us* to clearly see that the first thing we all want is the last thing we will ever need. The Bible leaves us no excuse to be ignorant about what's important, but we still can't seem to get it into our hearts and heads. So how is God left to reveal to us that His glory is worth more than the world's glory?

Suffering, in all of its various forms, is the point of contrast by which all good things are revealed. If you're like me, you rarely notice the moon in the early evening sky; but in the pitch black of night, it appears as a radiant and guiding light. In the same way, Jesus, the Light of the World, has always been shining, but the greatness of His glory was revealed to us against the darkest moment in history: the cross.

Like everyone else in the world, we do our best to escape suffering; even Jesus asked the Father to spare Him from the pain of His death. It's always easier to cling to comfort than to the cross, but the latter comes with far greater rewards. Ultimately, whether we go willingly or through a struggle, life *will* lead us into places of darkness, suffering, and death. If you haven't figured it out before you arrive in those places, you'll find out what's worth clinging on to when you get there.

On September 9, 2010, my wife, Sarah, gave birth to our first baby boy, Bowen Matthew Hammitt, at C. S. Mott Children's Hospital in Ann Arbor, Michigan. He was born with a rare and life-threatening congenital heart defect called hypoplastic left heart syndrome. At four days old, Bowen was taken to the operating room for his first open-heart surgery. We sat pensively in the waiting room for almost five hours before the surgeon came to tell us the surgery was successful.

That same night, on the morning of September 14, we received a call that jolted us out of our sleep. It was our nurse, and we heard panic in her voice. I'll never forget the time, 2:13 a.m., when we found out that Bowen's heart had stopped beating. Sarah and I rushed to his bedside as fast as we could, and we weren't prepared for what we saw. As we approached his bed, we saw one of Bowen's nurses with her fingers between the walls of his chest, pumping his heart to keep him alive. Sarah rested her head at Bowen's feet while I wrapped my arms around her and wept. We held his pale, cold fingers and toes while the doctors and nurses worked for over forty minutes to keep his heart beating. In those moments we felt certain we had lost our son, but by the grace of God and through the hands of a medical team, Bowen's life was saved.

My son's sternum was left open for several days after his surgery, and I had the experience of watching his heart beat between the open walls of his chest. On the day they closed "the window to his heart" (as we called it) I wrote the following paragraph in my journal:

> A friend told me that I've seen too much, but I'm realizing that I might not see enough. Everything I've watched happen in this hospital, all the pain I've felt, is deepening my faith, strengthening my marriage, and molding my character. As I lovingly stared into Bowen's eyes just before midnight, my face only

inches from his chest, I thought, "This love is an awe-some mess." I know I'm not the first person to think or to say something like that. Many great works of art have titles that are reminiscent of those words. I believe it's because tension is the place where the worst of life and the best of true hope meet to unveil our eyes to God's artistic work of redemption. What a mighty and creatively loving God we serve. He allows us to know great pain, so that we can know the greater pleasure of trading it in for purpose.

Sarah and I spent ten weeks in the hospital with Bowen, and during that time we came face-to-face with sickness, death, disease, and the emotional suffering of countless people within those walls. In a center of suffering, against a landscape of darkness, the light of the glory of God looked more radiant to me than I could have ever imagined, and I'm convinced that I've barely had a glimpse of its fullness.

God, in His loving and sovereign way, placed Palmer Chinchen in my life while Bowen was still in the hospital. If you've read his first book, *True Religion,* you know that Palmer is not afraid to march into the places of hell and suffering on earth, nor is he afraid to march you there with him. He leads his readers face-to-face with deep tragedy and pain, confronting the question *why?* without any fear of the answers. Palmer writes for a worthy cause that every one of us should take up with him: to break down the walls of our kingdoms of comfort in order to reveal and build up the kingdom of God on earth.

Scott Erickson

PART I

DARK NIGHTS

I'm convinced that God does His best work on dark canvas.

I say that because that's the picture painted in the opening pages of the Bible. God looked out on the vast darkness of the universe and splashed it with light and color and everything beautiful.

Then He picked up earth and hung it on the neck of the cosmos like a blue-sapphire and diamond pendant displayed on black silk behind locked glass. Some call it *the pale blue dot;* others, *the jewel of the universe.*

But what makes this world most stunning is life—your life. You are the miracle in the dark sky.

While in college in Southern California, my twin brother and I spent a weekend on the beaches south of Tijuana with a bunch of other college guys. On our way back we stopped in TJ to buy a few things that every college student brings back from Mexico:

switchblade combs, cherry bombs, ponchos … and a velvet paint-ing of Jennifer Beals. Paul bought her to hang in our dorm room. She was stunning. There was something about the soft, shimmering black fabric behind her that made her even more ravishing than she already was.

I wonder if life is a bit like that. When this world hurts us, fails us, and paints life black, we hate it. And sometimes we get lost swim-ming in the sea of darkness.

But maybe that darkness is only meant to be a backdrop that makes the portrait of your life more astonishing.

And when you stop to think about it, it seems like all things beautiful were once dark. The heavens were a deep black when God began to paint the skies. The day Jesus was crucified was dark as night, a striking contrast to His rising from death three days later on a bright Sunday morning. And the human heart is a dark cavern until the light of Christ transforms the soul.

Chapter 1

DARKNESS

Darkness is my closest friend.
Psalm 88:18

We have a saying in Africa: "God can't sleep."

Christmas is never supposed to be painful. Maybe that is one of the reasons the tragedy we experienced on the African Bible College campus in Lilongwe, Malawi, hurt so deeply. All fifty-three children from the ABC Christian Elementary Academy were lined up at the chapel door and had begun singing "Silent Night" as they entered, each carrying a lit candle.

Before the first child reached the decorated stage, I heard screams from the back of the room. When I turned, I saw several of the children's lamb costumes on fire. My brother and I grabbed a small girl running past us, on fire, and smothered the flames with our hands and bodies. I looked up and saw another girl, Damalise, fully ablaze. Several men had just backed away from her because her costume had exploded into a literal fireball.

Unfortunately, many of the parents had used a highly flammable glue, easily accessible in Malawi, to glue cotton balls on sheep costumes. As the kids waited in the back of the auditorium to begin the processional, some bumped into others with burning candles in hand, catching the lamb costumes on fire—and the costumes burned as if they'd been doused with gasoline.

I sprinted toward Damalise, pulled her to the ground. Strangely, I didn't feel any heat or pain as I plunged my hands into the flames. Several other men joined me to beat the flames out with our bare hands. All of us ended up with third-degree burns on our hands, arms, and necks. Several hours later, the pain that set in was excruciating.

But my burns were nothing compared to those that eleven-year-old Damalise sustained. Her skin was peeled back in large masses on her legs, arms, torso, and face. As her father and I carried her to the car, what she repeated over and over as she cried out in agony still echoes in my mind: "I'm going to die, I'm going to die." I tried to comfort her—"Damalise, you're not going to die." My words felt hollow.

Five children caught fire that December night. Four days later, Damalise went to heaven.

DARK GARDENS

From the very beginning of the Bible, the writers of Scripture used gardens to talk about life the way God meant it to be. Gardens represented all the beauty and goodness of God's presence.

The first garden was lush and green and filled with color, and God was everywhere. But then things went sideways; people (well, all two of them) turned on God, and they exchanged a flourishing garden for a dark desert. Eden was the Garden of Life, but people turned it into the Garden of Darkness.

The garden was still dark when Judas found Jesus in the garden of Gethsemane.[1] The Christ was beaten and hung on a Roman cross to suffocate. Heaven seemed silent. God seemed absent. Everyone wanted the angels to rush down from heaven and lift Him off the cross, but angels never came. He just hung there, in the heat, sweating and bleeding … to death.

He was buried in a garden as the first day turned to night.[2]

We all want to rush to the end of the story, the third day, because this story has to get better, brighter … but that's not how God meant this life to be. The first day, the dark day, is a day everyone must live. For some the darkness seems to last a lifetime.

Christians often act as though we can live in such a way that the darkness won't touch us. But the world God put us in just doesn't work that way.

Life hurts.

Pain is real.

Suffering surrounds us.

GOD, IT HURTS

Yesterday Pamela came to my office; she said she wanted to tell me about her pain. She told me she was raped when she was seventeen. Now, more than fifteen years later, she still hurts. God, it hurts!

How can God sleep at night when there is so much pain in this world? If God loves people as deeply as the Bible says, and if God has all the power in the universe, then why in the world do the very worst things happen to the very best people? Why are beautiful seventeen-year-old girls attacked by filthy men? Why!?

All of us ask these ringing questions on life's dark nights, on nights when children dressed as innocent lambs sing about the birth of God's Son, then burn to death. How in the world can this happen? Is God asleep?

THE DARK CONTINENT

Several years ago I took a leave from the pastorate to teach at a Christian college in the African country of Malawi. When I arrived, I was shocked by the widespread suffering. Sickness and diseases like malaria and AIDS were rampant. Poverty littered the landscape. Nowhere else—not even elsewhere in Africa, where I have traveled widely—had I seen grown men walk barefoot on city streets. The living conditions were unsanitary; hunger turned to starvation; children wore soiled rags for clothes.

As I lived through this experience, I began looking for biblical answers to the problems of pain, suffering, and injustice. I also realized that I didn't have a well-thought-out, articulated theology of pain. We say really cheap things like, "God won't give you more than you can handle." The Bible doesn't say that. Let's be honest—suffering does not fit well in the framework of Western Christianity.

In the middle of these explorations, I began writing material for a course I would teach called "A Theology of Suffering." Later, when I taught the course, my students and I wrestled with the problem of pain. We read books, we searched Scripture for answers, and we talked about the culprits of injustice. The process was refreshing and eye-opening.

In our search, we read Brennan Manning's *The Ragamuffin Gospel.* Manning's signature book wonderfully describes how Jesus spent a disproportionate amount of time with people who had been damaged along the dark paths of life: the lame, the blind, the downtrodden, the lepers, the tired, the broken, and the lost.[3]

We discussed Henri Nouwen's *The Wounded Healer,* in which Nouwen explains that Jesus lived a wounded life, but that through His wounds, you and I are made whole. His wounds were the very price of our healing.[4] And here's the beauty of it: The Wounded One is among us today. He sits with you on lonely days. He cries with you through dark nights.

My students were also intrigued by the blunt honesty of Shusaku Endo's magnificent novel *Silence.*[5] Endo describes the feelings of doubt, disappointment, and frustration with God that all people feel when pain seems unbearable. We've all been there, but we seldom feel like we can be honest about it.

And we read C. S. Lewis' short classic *The Problem of Pain.* The creator of Narnia forced us to wrestle with the sovereign power of God. He caused us to explore the depth of God's love. He also opened our eyes to the sad reality that, as long as we live in a world filled with people, the possibility of pain is always present. People want to blame God for affliction, yet so often people are the cause of some of life's greatest pain: a cheating husband, an abusive parent, guns, car bombs, genocide, torture, manipulation, oppressive governments, and greed.[6]

Initially I believed the course would have its greatest application in the developing world. Yet after returning to the pastorate in the United States, my eyes were opened to the reality of what we all deal with: the death of a child, the ravage of cancer, the devastation of a failing marriage and a broken family, the hopeless feeling of being unemployed, a foreclosed home, financial failure.

My conviction hit home when I received a phone call about a family we knew—they had found their two-year-old son at the bottom of their swimming pool.

I walked into intensive care to see a beautiful blond, curly headed toddler lifeless in his father's strong arms. Tears leaked silently from the father's eyes as a machine kept his son's heart beating.

What do you say in a moment like that? Where was God? What is my answer to this?

Where do we get the notion that we, as Christians, are supposed to behave as though we are immune to tragedy and, when there is catastrophe, to act like it was painless? As though suffering would imply we have lost faith in God.

As prevalent as suffering is, most Western Christians have little or no theological framework to deal with pain. The messiness of pain simply doesn't fit with polished shopping malls, granite countertops, and cushioned pews. Preachers, authors, and professors avoid the subject.

Those who do attempt to address the idea of pain end up saying the trite things we've heard before: "It must be God's will," or "It's okay; God is in control." The truth is, pain goes deep, and answers are elusive.

My challenge to you, as you read this book, is to formulate a Christian response to suffering. Wrestle with the questions all people ask: "Where is God when life hurts?" "How long will I stay in the darkness?" "Why me, God? Why—when the world is filled with bad people—why would you allow me to be hurt so deeply?"

I recently asked three short questions of the people at our church, The Grove: "If you have been affected by cancer, please stand. If you have lived through or are living in a broken family, please stand. If you are economically desperate or without a job, please stand."

Practically the entire room, for three consecutive services, stood. We've all been hit. We're all left standing, barely.

Trouble

travels

fast.

Suffering is the world's common language. People everywhere know what it means to hurt. The Bible begins with a story of pain and ends with a failing planet. The question is not, "Will we face suffering?" but, "When?" We all make mistakes; we all have relationships that sour; we all age and have more aches and pains by the day.

I don't have pat or simple answers for you. I hope to not say anything glib. But I do invite you to sit, be silent, and discover what God has for you in life's dark nights.

This book is for everyone who has ...

> lost a job
> moved out of state
> been sick
> had a teenager rebel
> cried
> been lost in love
> filed for bankruptcy
> sat alone
> crashed a car
> lost a father
> ended a marriage
> managed a blended family
> slipped into debt ... lots of it
> or watched their future wither and dreams fade.

This book is for you.

IN THE NIGHT

Now my story is told,
Opened book, pages to unfold,
My story is true, though seemingly old,
Remember it …
In the night.

A dusky light calls,
As the sun's face falls,
My friends and I will crawl,
Over shadows …
In the night.

A vanishing distant scream,
Rumbling behind the trees,
Rustling with the leaves,
Beyond the wall …
In the night.

Stomach filled, but soul left empty,
Wandering forever in a naked purgatory,
Family and friends remaining memory,
All else is gone …
In the night.

Here I am, this lonely wanderer,
Roaming through fall, winter, spring and summer,

Maybe, in this world there still is another,

Hope there is ...

In the night.[7]

E. A. Melville

Chapter 2

BOULEVARD OF BROKEN DREAMS

The Lord is close to the brokenhearted.
Psalm 34:18

It's after midnight, and the Kenyan border guard won't budge. He insists our documents are invalid and says we'll have to sort out our problems with a customs official in the morning.

Namanga is a dirty, shack-filled, dilapidated town on the Tanzania-Kenya border. My son, three college students from Arizona, and I have already spent fifteen hours in the van getting here. The last thing any of us wants is to spend the night in it. I walk up and down the narrow streets of Namanga, looking for something resembling a motel. Nothing even close. There are a few noisy bars, lorry drivers drinking beer on curbs or sleeping under their semis—but no motels. I've always felt comfortable in Africa, having lived there for nearly twenty years, but this particularly dark night in Namanga doesn't feel right.

I begin to tell the guys we'll be sleeping with one eye open in the now mosquito-infested van when a young man walks up and asks if we need a place to sleep. All evening we have been shooing away street vendors trying to sell us everything from bubble gum to jumper cables, but this guy seems different. The first thing I notice is his ear lobe, which is looped into a knot through a large hole in his skin—a mark of the Maasai. But he has on street clothes, not their traditional tunic with beads. He's also much shorter than other Maasai I had met.

"Are you Maasai?" I venture.

"Yes," he answers with a smile. "How did you know?"

The Maasai are a warrior tribe. Historically, Maasai rites of passage require a boy to kill a lion. They are known throughout eastern Africa for their uncompromising integrity and unequaled courage. Expatriates in Nairobi or Dar es Salaam all desire Maasai for night watchmen. You'll find them throughout the cities, standing guard in traditional clothing, wearing a massive string of beads and dangling earrings, a spear in hand. Quite simply, you don't mess with Maasai.

"Just a wild guess," I answer.

He proceeds to tell us that just on the other side of the Kenyan gate is a beautiful resort. "Your van must stay here, but we can walk to the resort. It's very close," the Maasai assures us.

It sounds better than the van. Two from our group agree to brave the mosquitoes and thieves and sleep in the van while the remaining three of us, with the Maasai as our new guide, head off on foot. We pass a few seedy bars, slip under the guard gate dividing Kenya and Tanzania, and head up a deserted path into the Kenyan darkness.

And when I say darkness, I mean dark as a tomb! As we stumble down the road I ask, half mumbling, "If there's a resort, where are the lights?"

"The generator must be out of diesel," our Maasai asserts with confidence.

Convenient, I think, and add aloud, "Well, how far is it?"

"Oh, it's close, very close," he says.

Now I really begin to smell a setup. I'm certain we're about to be jumped, beat down, and robbed. Slowing my pace, I whisper to one of the college students, a woodsman/Green Beret/wannabe automatic-weapons expert: "John, do you have your knife on you?"

"No," he says sheepishly.

"What? Are you kidding me?" I nearly shout back.

This guy loves weapons. He takes knives and guns to McDonald's. I begin to think we're finished, done for.

It has somehow gotten even darker than the tomb dark from before; I cannot see ten feet in front of me.

"Maasai, we're turning around," I say at last.

"No, no, we're almost there," he assures me. "Trust me, this is a beautiful resort."

"Trust him," John says. "He's Maasai."

I want to trust him, I do, but it's dark and he's short. Maasai are supposed to be tall. Plus he's wearing jeans and a T-shirt instead of the traditional red plaid wrap. I keep looking at his knotted ear lobe for comfort. *Okay, keep going, keep going.*

Finally we reach an unlit, unmarked building with high walls, and I begin to feel some relief when suddenly a tall figure slips from behind the tree to my right. He's holding a spear in one hand and a machete in the other and coming toward us quickly …

I'll tell you how this all turns out when we get to part III.

The Bible is filled with stories of God's people walking dark paths:

- Abraham spent three long nights on the dark path to Moriah, where he was supposed to kill his own son.
- In the dark of night, Moses led a band of runaway slaves down the road out of Egypt.
- David fled down the desert path to Adullam and ended up in a dark cave because his king wanted him dead.
- Saul's world turned pitch black on the road to Damascus.
- And on one dark afternoon, even the Christ was made to drag His cross down dusty streets in Jerusalem.

Life has paths like that: dark. Dark as Egypt … or Namanga. And we hate to walk them. But here's what I hope you understand—there's a kind of spirituality that grows only in the dark. You see, God uses the dark and difficult days to mature us spiritually in a way that won't happen on the days when the sun shines and the flowers bloom.

So walk the broken roads; go down the dark paths. God is growing you.

BOULEVARD OF BROKEN DREAMS

A month after Hurricane Katrina struck its savage blow on the Gulf Coast, I made my way to Biloxi, Mississippi, seeking pastors and churches that our church, The Grove, could partner with to provide assistance.

As we slowly made our way to the coast, inching around rubble and teams of people cleaning debris from the streets, we saw obvious damage, but nothing to overwhelm us. That is, until we rounded the brick walls of the First Presbyterian Church and caught our first glimpse of the ocean … and the real devastation.

The contrast was surreal. It was a balmy Mississippi morning. The sky was blue; the Gulf's green water splashed lazily onto the white sand. My eyes went to the beach first, as eyes tend to do—always attracted to beauty.

But then I glanced left and right; nothing but sheer devastation as far as the eye could see. Rubble everywhere—piles of it. Houses had collapsed on each other. Bedsheets hung from trees fifty feet above the ground. Cars washed onto rooftops.

Just then I noticed an elderly couple picking through the debris. All that was left of their home, which had once stood just a few dozen feet from the church, were their concrete front steps. Nothing—absolutely nothing else—remained. The couple didn't speak, and in their grave silence, they picked and dug through the sparse rubble, hoping to find some remnant of a life that was now a flickering memory.

We climbed back into our car and turned east down Beach Boulevard, a highway typically filled with tourists heading to the beach. But that day was different. Beach Boulevard was broken.

Concrete sections of road were torn apart and piled on top of one another. In many places, whole chunks of the highway were completely gone, washed out to sea or smashed into someone's living room.

As we drove, the devastation continued for miles. We never reached the end; it seemed as though there wasn't one. Eerily, the town's playground was shrouded in thousands of strands of shredded clothing, pulled and left there by the raging waters, stripped into rags by the violent wind. We passed an entire family sitting on concrete steps leading up to what used to be a grand beachfront home. They sat in silence, weeping. I almost stopped to offer comfort but sensed the privacy of the moment, their moment to mourn.

Before turning inland, we passed one last reminder of where we were. On a large fractured piece of plywood that leaned against a tree were four words, spray-painted in red:

BOULEVARD OF BROKEN DREAMS

And that's what it was.

Life is like that, a journey filled with beauty and pain. We meander along, wishing for only sunny days on the beach, but then a storm strikes. Our passage is rudely interrupted. Skies turn dark, clouds move in, and the placid world we have known is shattered by a broken promise, a lost job, a damaged marriage, a financial mess, a sick child, a lost loved one.

Affliction will come in many forms and at the most unexpected moments. The reality of living in a fallen and sinful world is that life will hurt, and we will have gray days and dark nights filled with pain.

Pain is real, and it hurts.

DENIAL

Why is it that we are so ashamed of our troubles? Why does our culture cause us to want to hide our affliction like a leper hides his sores? We mask our pain with glassy smiles or drown it with addictions. Deep down we believe that nobody wants a friend with problems, so we live in denial of our trouble and act like it doesn't hurt.

Our society fosters a false sense of security unequaled in any other place or time. Children are raised to believe they possess an inalienable right to live free of harm. Precautions are taken to protect people from the most obscure and trite dangers. Practically every product imaginable on the market provides warnings and instructions on how to avoid harmful exposure or use. From warning labels on coffee cups to safety instructions for infant cribs, there is virtually no risk we are not warned against. And yet our obsession with protectionism has not only become absurd but has proved futile.

I think Christians are often in greater denial of affliction than non-Christians because we almost feel we should be immune.

I had known the Wilsons (not their actual names) all of their years working as missionaries in Africa. They lived just two miles from my home, so it hurt deeply the morning we learned of the tragic deaths.

Sara and her twelve-year-old daughter, Chelsea, remained home while her husband, Jeff, and younger son traveled to the capital city.

That night, a man the family knew well entered the home, and Sara woke up to the sounds of her daughter resisting his attempts to rape her. Sara charged into the bedroom to defend her. But the man had taken a butcher knife from the kitchen. Sara was strong and fought long and hard. Blood stained the floors and the walls in the three rooms. He killed them both.

We were all sick. It was as dark as tragedies get. Yet what stuck with me most was that neither Jeff nor his ten-year-old son would cry. (Even after the shock wore off.) At the time, I perceived their catatonic state as an attempt to be spiritually stoic. I didn't get it. They were in complete denial that this sickening tragedy hurt—as though if God is real then pain is not.

It just isn't that way.

I remember one of my high school friends, the Wilsons' next-door neighbor, telling me that this horrific murder was God's will. I told him I disagreed. We argued for a long time. I told him there's no way I can say that this awful, senseless act came from God. I don't care how many Old Testament verses you read to me. He got really mad.

The sovereignty of God is a tough thing. Because if God is all good and all powerful at the same time, then why in the world would he allow the twelve-year-old daughter of missionaries to be raped and stabbed to death?

The killer was caught the next day while trying to leave the country, wearing Jeff's clothes. Jeff went down to the prison and told him he forgave him. Wow, I didn't get that either. I know what the Bible says about forgiveness, but I'm just being honest with you. I felt nothing but rage. The wounds were too fresh. I did feel slightly vindicated a number of months later when rebel soldiers overran the police station and killed the murderer.

God catches up; that's why we say in Liberia, "God can't sleep."

LIFE'S POTHOLES OF PAIN

Driving on African roads is always an adventure. The military checkpoints are some of the many menacing obstacles, but the most ominous are the countless deep, wide, hidden potholes. Just when you think you can cruise at seventy, you'll round a corner and slam into a two-foot-deep, six-foot-wide, mud-filled pothole that will jar your teeth, rattle your bones, and crack your axle in two.

Last week I rode two hundred numbing miles through Liberia in a van with twenty basketball players and musicians from The Grove. It's rainy season, so the potholes are even bigger. We sloshed and bounced for eight hours! Joel described the drive as his own private hell.

The boulevard of life is like that. It's a broken road filled with cracks and potholes. You may swerve and miss a few, but eventually you'll hit a deep one that will jolt your soul and stop you in your tracks.

WHEN PAIN GETS PHYSICAL

When I was in college, I learned that my kidney was significantly blocked, so my doctor scheduled a procedure to have a catheter inserted. At the time I felt pretty good and gladly headed into the hospital basement (or should I say torture chamber?) to have a technician insert the thing. I had absolutely no clue what I was in for.

The young man, it seemed, had never implanted a catheter into a kidney ... successfully. Brandishing a six-inch needle, he stabbed—I mean inserted—it into my side, with no anesthesia, mind you (I assumed they wanted me conscious for the ensuing interrogation). However, three inches in, the needle bent. The pain was excruciating. So he pulled it out and started over. The second time, once again, it bent. Through my shameless groaning, I heard him mumble something about my skin being too tough and that he needed more leverage. Still conscious, I watched him climb onto the gurney and straddle my abdomen on his knees—I'm pretty sure this is not how the procedure was taught in medical school!

After finally getting the needle into my kidney (it could have been my spleen for all I knew!), he proceeded to tell me that this was the first of three needles to be inserted into my kidney before the catheter itself. The word *pain* at this point seems awfully shallow to fully express what I was feeling.

This example, however, fails to do justice to the physically debilitating pain many struggle with daily. By comparison, my kidney experience is like a scraped knee from a playground fall. The pain was temporary, and I healed quickly. And yet in a small way, I was able to get a sense of how awful physical pain can be. What I experienced for half a day is a daily experience for many who fight chronic disease and disabilities. For them, every day is filled with agonizing physical affliction. I think of those fighting daily with diabetes, cancer, or AIDS. Or those struggling with multiple sclerosis or Parkinson's, or those recovering from a stroke or paralysis. They know pain intimately, and it hurts.

LOST

One of the perks of pastoring in Arizona is that swimming pools are deemed a necessity. I love time together with my four sons in the pool after work or on the weekends. But throughout the many years we have reared our sons—all of them good swimmers—I never overcame the fear of one of my sons drowning. Every summer the news stations keep a running total of the number of victims who drown in the Phoenix area—a heart-numbing statistic. One instance that sticks in my mind is the story of a fireman father who had his two-year-old in the garage with him while he was woodworking. Distracted momentarily by his task, the father failed to notice his son wander out of the garage and open a partially closed side gate to the pool. Ten minutes later, when the father noticed his son was missing, it was too late.

Loss is unquestionably one of life's most painful experiences. We are left with a void in our lives that cannot be filled. The suddenness of the event alone can leave a person in a state of deep, shocked grief. Stunned, they struggle to move on.

After losing her husband of more than fifty years, a wife expressed her pain to me like this: "I feel like half a person." Loss of a spouse who moves out cuts almost as deep. Losing a friend who moves out of state really hurts. Losing your children to a nasty divorce is bitter. Even losing a job you love leaves you feeling hollow and worthless. The pain of loss is a lingering sorrow that can last a lifetime.

PEOPLE HURT PEOPLE

Relational struggles inflict some of life's deepest wounds. C. S.
Lewis explains in *The Problem of Pain*, "The possibility of pain is
inherent in the very existence of a world where souls can meet.
When souls become wicked they will certainly use this possibility
to hurt one another."[1] Just as surely as we will encounter physical
pain, we also will be hurt by people we know and love. Relational
pain often comes in the form of a crumbling marriage, unfaithfulness, a rebellious child, financial pressures, or conflict in the
workplace.

God created humanity to enjoy the love and friendship shared in
relationships—with Him and with those around us. We are relational
vacuums, thriving on the interaction we have with one another, in
families, in friendships, and even at work. However, life is certain to
throw at us relational conflicts that can rip our hearts out.

I recently ran into my friend Phil, whom I had not seen in several
years. Upon recognizing him, I blurted out, "Phil! How are you?"

What a glib question. We tend to ask these immense existential
questions of people when in reality all we want is a simple, "I'm fine,
thanks, and you?"

So of course I was caught completely off guard when he told the
truth. "Terrible," he said. As I sat down and listened, Phil told me
about his wife's decision to leave him. Unwilling to seek reconcilia-
tion, she had filed for divorce. She had grown tired and restless in
the monotony of marriage and was seeing another man, also married
with children, and whose wife had filed for divorce because of his
infidelity. The next day Phil was to appear in court because his wife
was requesting sole custody of their two young sons.

Phil's voice shook, his eyes watered. The agony he was experiencing was etched across his face as his entire being was tearing apart. Phil was walking through a valley darker than I could imagine.

The relational pain we experience in life is real, and it deeply hurts. And surprisingly, it's often the people we love the most who wound us the deepest. It may be a husband or wife, it may be a coworker who turns on us, it may be a friend who wreaks havoc on your life with words—filling your days with conflict and misery. You may have a son- or a daughter-in-law who is hurting you deeply. It may be a member of your church, a fellow Christian, who has slandered your name, attacked your character, and stolen your peace. A retiring pastor just told me, "My staff have caused my deepest wounds."

MARGINALIZED

A less noticeable form that pain takes is the suffering caused by the unjust treatment of people. Racism, injustice, and poverty are just a few ways in which people can be hurt by society. For many people, these are non-issues. In the daily bubble of mall shopping, soccer practice, and American Idol, many of us never feel the sting of discrimination in the workplace, or feel the helplessness of being unable to quiet the hunger pangs of our families. Yet many people live every day under a cloud of racism, discrimination, injustice, and oppression.

A growing problem in suburban America is child prostitution. Some better refer to it as child sex slavery. Young teenagers are recruited in malls and from in front of movie theaters. My friend Pat, who leads BrandedPHX's efforts to eradicate child prostitution, says the average age a girl enters prostitution is thirteen. He tells the story of a junior-high girl named Katie who was persuaded to go to a pimp's house. When she walked in, he tied her up and put her in a cage. This is right here in Phoenix, Arizona. Not Thailand or Somalia. She was sold out of the cage for a month before vice officers finally tracked her down and set her free.

It doesn't have to be this way. You and I can make a difference. We can love the marginalized, defend the oppressed, feed the hungry, stop discrimination, and set the prisoners free. Jesus said that when we do this for others, we do this for Him.

Years ago the Hebrew prophet Isaiah told us to give our lives to freeing people like Katie: "Loose the chains of injustice and untie the cords of the yoke, to set the oppressed free.... Share your food with the hungry and ... provide the poor wanderer with shelter.... Clothe [the naked].... Then your light will rise in the darkness, and your night will become like the noonday." [2]

Life is a broken road. For some the road becomes too much to bear. The constant jarring and unexpected turns drain their souls. They give up somewhere along the way. They give up on love, they give up on their futures, they give up on God. But know this: It's God's road for your life. And you don't walk alone. The Christ walks with you.

He walks with you today because He knows what it's like to walk down dark paths. So before He left He said—like His Father always said—*I will be with you.* You see, on a dark afternoon about two thousand years ago, He was made to drag His own cross down the dusty streets of Jerusalem and up a rugged hill to a place called Golgotha—the place of the skull. It was a place of death. But the path was rough and the cross was heavy, so His feet slowed—He knew this road led to death. But then God sent an African named Simon to walk with Him and share the load. I think the dark road turned a bit brighter, because He no longer walked alone.

Neither do you.

FADE

Tears at the edge of my heart,
screaming and fighting to break free.
To escape from this pain that never ends,
always suffocating me till I feel nothing.

An empty garden of ash, now replaces my murdered
emotions that for so long have suffered endlessly.
So alone within myself is bad enough,
and now I got the future to face alone too.
So many nights, I've spent drowning in a pool
of alcohol, pills, hate, blood and memories.
Destroying myself for every little mistake I've made,
Just left to bleed it out in confusion and nightmares

When will reality wake me up,
everywhere and everyone feels like an enemy,
all I ever see is the past and I'm rushed with fear....
So long I've slept in the arms of depression
and hurting away every piece of who I am.
My image is wasted and broken, it's so unbearable
to not want to smash any mirror I stand in front of.
To see my ugly face, the scars that remain, the eyes
that see nothing but darkness...[3]

Darkys Black

Chapter 3

DARK NIGHT OF THE SOUL

He makes me dwell in darkness.
Psalm 143:3

Young and in love, Brad and Alisha moved to California to start their life together. She was beautiful and full of promise. He was lazy and couldn't hold a job. While she went to work, he stayed home, forming new addictions. First the habits seemed minor—alcohol, pornographic magazines. But the addictions multiplied like cockroaches in the sewer. Soon every addiction you can name had a grip on Brad's life. Theft, infidelity, drugs—he had them all.

He was a mess when he showed up at Alisha's workplace. He followed her down the aisles, ranting in a meth tirade, demanding money. But she had cut him off. She was sick of the mess he had made of their lives and refused to feed his obsessions any longer.

She tried to ignore him. She hoped the store's security would come to her rescue. They didn't. He grabbed her by the hair and dragged her out the door. Security showed up but just stood in the doorway and watched, later claiming their responsibility ended at the franchise entrance.

Cowards. I can't stand cowards.

Brad dragged Alisha to his car and forced her in. Witnesses in the parking lot were too afraid of the crazed maniac to intervene. As he sped out of the parking lot, he yanked a handful of hair out of Alisha's head. Blood covered her face.

Pulling onto the freeway, he screamed, "I'm going to kill you!" He meant it.

With the car now careening down the freeway at over a hundred miles an hour, Alisha was his prisoner to the death. Spotting an off-ramp, he yanked the car to the right and straight up the steep incline toward the freeway overpass, never letting up on the gas.

I've driven under the overpass; it's higher than most, a good seventy-five feet above the freeway below.

As Brad raced up the off-ramp, he aimed the car straight through the guardrails at the top … and launched the car off the overpass.

Alisha prayed. That's all she could do.

The car landed nose first in the freeway median and rolled. Immediately passersby stopped to help. Miraculously Alisha was able to climb out of the crumpled car and ran toward the first couple she saw, shouting, "Save me, save me, he's trying to kill me!"

Brad looked dead. The first paramedics on the scene thought he was dead. He's not. He's in prison.

I wish he was dead—I'm just being honest with you.

I know Alisha well. She's beautiful, and rage runs through my veins when I think about what happened to her on that dark Nevada night.

But God can't sleep. He says, "Vengeance is Mine."

Why do two-year-olds swipe toys from other two-year-olds—then bite their noses?

Why do fast-food workers at drive-throughs always short you one bag of fries?

Why are mechanics' bills always twice their estimate?

Why do Olympic snowboarders try an indy grab that causes them to crash when the finish line is just fifty yards away?

There's this thing called sin. And it's a problem, a bigger problem than you think. It's a problem because sin turns life dark. It darkens life on the inside and causes us to live dark lives. Sin robs us of happiness, it ruins relationships, it fills us with shame, it destroys our futures, and it distances us from God. Your soul will turn dark. Richard Rohr calls it the dark night of the soul.[1]

That's why I say your sin problem is bigger than you think.

It used to be that Christians were deeply bothered by sin. It used to be that pastors and parents warned about the dangers of sin. Now it seems that people grin about sin like an inside joke. Some behave like almost nothing is wrong anymore. But sin is serious business with God. It will mess up your life.

This is one piece of doctrine we like to forget. Some picture God as a gray-headed gentleman who cannot bear the thought of punishing people He loves ... but the raw truth is, sin bothers God.

Sometimes we don't think our sin problem is very big.

Jesus illustrates this problem when He tells the story of two men praying. The first is a religious leader, who stands on a street corner and prays, "God, I thank you that I'm not like the rest of the people gathered here—the robbers, the evildoers, the adulterers. And all the people standing around listening to me pray. I'm not even like that guy right there, that tax collector."[2]

The Pharisee never sees his own sin problem.

If you are trying to live with sin in your life ... it's a bigger problem than you think. It will turn you dark on the inside.

This was the case with Israel soon after the people crossed into Canaan. As their armies took control of the region, God gave one simple command: Take no loot. But the temptation was too much for one soldier named Achan. He swiped some booty (life lesson: Booty will always get you in trouble) and buried it in his backyard.

Israel's next conquest was to take control of a small city named Ai. Joshua knew the battle should be an easy win, so he sent just a fraction of his warriors. But Israel's sin problem was bigger than he thought. God would not go with them. Ai took them down hard.

When they finally came back to God to ask why He would allow them to be defeated by tiny Ai, He said, "Your sin problem is bigger than you think. You have sin in the camp, and until that sin is gone, I'll be gone too."[3]

My dad often says, "Where sin is, God isn't."

It hardly made sense—a nation suffers for one man's sin. It's so small, so insignificant. Who would notice? It was just a jacket and some bling.

But Achan was the fly in the ointment, the sand in the crankshaft, the floater in the lemonade. God would not be on their side until Achan was dealt with. Their sin problem was bigger than they thought.

We had a long layover in Brussels on our way home from Liberia last month and were hanging out in Starbucks when Nils said, "Man, my toe really hurts."

"I'm a doctor, let me take a look." I know I'm the wrong kind of doctor, the kind that can't help you when you're sick, but we had a long layover.

So Nils took his sock off in Starbucks and showed me the thing. "Wow, it's rotten!" I exclaimed.

He had had a blister pop in his work boots, and now it was infected, very infected. The gaping wound was black, and his entire foot, going up his ankle, was red—a sure sign the infection was spreading, headed toward his heart! He hadn't paid much attention to the popped blister. It was just a blister, just a sore toe. No big deal. But now it was a real problem.

"I don't know much about infections, Nils, but get that thing checked as soon as you get back," I warned.

Two days later he was in the hospital. His toe problem was bigger than he thought.

THE PROBLEM WITH SIN
Sin is Dumb

Mike was a bright, personable, progressive pastor at a very large church, led highly successful ministries for years, was respected in the community, and had a beautiful wife and kids. But then something changed in him. He became a difficult person and jumped from one church to the next before ending up managing a fast-food restaurant.

He soon found the easy access to cash too tempting to pass. He stole thousands and thousands of dollars. Working with dozens of young college students also presented its own brand of temptation. He soon started to sleep with the young women who worked for him.

Some of his staff began offering him cocaine. He tried it and liked it, and there was plenty more cash in the register to feed his new habit.

Then everyone found out. His wife found out, the franchise found out, the police found out.

How in the world did life spiral into such a dark abyss?

Sin.

Sin is dumb.

Sin will mess you up.

The wrong and evil in this world, what the Bible names *sin*, will ruin your life. We think we can play with it, dabble in it, ignore it … it will mess up your life.

Sin festers; it grows and spreads like a topical infection in your toe, and it heads straight for your heart.

The sheer foolishness of sin will ruin your life. Sin has this way of making us do really dumb things.

Sin is dumb.

I know a guy who had a promising and growing career at a university, but he was just fired because he stole a box of Xerox paper. Dumb.

Recently a governor told his wife and family he was leaving to hike the Appalachian Trail. Instead he got on a plane and flew to Argentina to meet his girlfriend. Dumber.

During a college spring break, I stayed in the dorm at Biola to work. Bored one afternoon, I heard the shower down the hall turn on. In a moment of brilliance, I remembered the cherry bombs we had bought in Tijuana. I crept into the bathroom, lit the huge firecracker and lobbed it over the shower curtain like a live grenade.

The ceramic-tiled bathroom made it sound like a bomb went off. The guy started screaming like a little girl, so I ran back to my dorm room. Our resident director came up, knocked at my door, and asked if I was the one who threw a stick of dynamite into the shower. You see, it was spring break, and there were only two guys on our floor: me and the guy whose ears were bleeding. Really dumb.

The RD looked at me and said, "Why? Why did you do it?"

I didn't know why. Who knows why? There was no *why*. There was no deep, meaningful reason behind my actions. None of us really knows why; that's why I say the foolishness of sin will ruin your life.

But life is like that. No one decides one day, "I'm going to do something really messed up and ruin my life." We don't; it just happens that way.

> No one gets married with plans to keep a mistress in Argentina.
> No one loses her temper knowing it will cost her job.
> No one has kids with plans to ignore them because he or she is a workaholic.

So my warning in all this is, if you want to really mess your life up … live with sin. If you want to remain distant from God … live with sin.

Sin is Addictive

Sin will mess up your life because it's so addictive. Nobody commits single sins.

Like the gangs of LA do drive-bys, we do walk-bys. It's like catching a whiff of Cinnabon at the mall. You think, *I'm just going to walk by and see if they're as fresh as they smell.* But as you get close, you're sucked right in like a fly to honey. *I'll just get a couple of mini-bons … for the kids*, you reason. *I need to do it for the kids.* But the sales staff smell your weakness; they up-sell you. Now you're loaded down with a dozen big ones … with extra frosting on the side.

You think about keeping a couple for the kids, but you've DVRed three episodes of *America's Got Talent,* so you just bury the empty box in the neighbor's trash can.

Addiction is crafty, confusing, compelling, powerful, and greedy. It reproduces and spreads like a cancer. You give it an inch; it wants a mile.

Sin is patient.[4] The addiction of sin waits for you. It will hang around like a gnat in summer, for years. Then one day it will lock its jaws on you like a piranha.

In his metaphysical classic, *The Great Divorce,* C. S. Lewis describes sin as a red lizard.

> I saw coming toward us a Ghost who carried something on his shoulder.… What sat on his shoulder was a little red lizard, and it was twitching its tail like a whip and whispering things in his ear.…
>
> "Would you like me to make him quiet?" said the flaming Spirit—an angel.…
>
> "Of course I would," said the Ghost.
>
> "Then I will kill him," said the Angel.…
>
> "Keep away," said the Ghost.…
>
> "Don't you *want* him killed?"
>
> "You didn't say anything about *killing* him at first. I hardly meant to bother you with anything so drastic as that."
>
> "It's the only way," said the Angel.… "Shall I kill it?"
>
> "… I was only thinking about silencing it."
>
> "May I kill it?"

"Well, there's time to discuss that later."

"There is no time. May I kill it?"

"... Please—really—don't bother.... Thanks ever so much."

"May I kill it?

"... I think the gradual process would be far better than killing it."

"The gradual process is of no use at all."

"... Some other day, perhaps."

"There is no other day ..."

"... How can I tell you to kill it? You'd kill *me* if you did."

"... I never said it wouldn't hurt you. I said it wouldn't kill you."

"... Let me run back by to-night's bus and get an opinion from my own doctor."

"This moment contains all moments.... I cannot kill it against your will."[5]

Too many of us live like that. We think we can live with our sins. We think they won't bother us too much. But secrets and sin slowly kill the soul.

Satan is the lord of addictions. He relishes addiction because he knows it puts him in control. The writers of the Bible knew this, so they warn us with words like, "Our struggle is not against flesh and blood, but against the rulers, against the authorities, against the powers of this dark world and against the spiritual forces of evil in the heavenly realms." [6]

Sin Ruins People

Sin always has relational consequences. It started in the garden; sin ruined Adam and Eve's relationship with God. Like venom from a spitting cobra, sin spews and hurts everyone near you.

Gossip, for example, destroys friendships. Alcohol breaks down families. Anger costs us our jobs. Sin always comes with a price; there's always collateral damage. You never sin in a vacuum.

Here's a sad truth: Families transmit sins. Children repeat the sins of their parents. Children raised in abusive homes are the most likely adults to be abusive parents. Most alcoholics had alcoholic parents. Slothful parents will raise lazy kids.

Do you see why I say sin will mess up your life?

MERCY ME

Earlier in this chapter I talked about two pray-ers. The first, the Pharisee, couldn't see his sin problem to save his life.

The second pray-er worked for the IRS. People didn't like him. He knew he was a low-down cheat and a scoundrel. He had no scruples. But he did know his sin problem was big.

So when he prays, he begs, "Have mercy on me, a sinner."[7]

He begs for mercy.

Life will fill with junk. We hide secrets, compile lies, form addictions, and take what does not belong to us. Nobody wants to talk about the junk in life. Who needs that? But the truth is we all carry junk. It weighs us down. It makes life heavy. It ruins relationships. It pulls us away from God. And until we are honest about the wrong, until we beg for mercy, life will be dark.

If you stick with Lewis' story about the red lizard, the man finally asks for help. He pleads for mercy. The lizard is not slain but transformed into a beautiful white stallion, which the man mounts and rides away.

"Have *mercy* on me for I am a sinner."

It's all about mercy.

SADNESS

trying hard to keep the tears from flowing
there's a hole
it goes deep down inside of me
sick!
and alone!
the tears....
come at night!
aching....
bleeding in the full moon's light!
blood mixed with tears ...
no one knows
what goes on
behind these eyes![8]

Andy

Chapter 4

SILENT NIGHTS

*My God, I cry out by day, but you do not
answer, by night, and am not silent.*
Psalm 22:2

I have a friend from South Africa here in Arizona. He's dying. When he was a young engineer working in Cape Town, he was exposed to toxic chemicals. The toxins have started to destroy his bone marrow. He has three great kids and a wonderful wife; they all just got back from vacationing in Puerto Rico. He looks great on the outside, but his insides are killing him.

Why? Where is God?

When life hurts, or when tragedy strikes, our first response is often, "Where is God?" Or, "Why in the world did God let this happen?" We turn on God, feeling disappointment with Him for

His apparent willingness to allow us to suffer. Is God merciless? Is God impotent?

Is God silent?

Shusaku Endo's piercing novel *Silence* recounts the persecution of the seventeenth-century church in Japan. The book wrestles with a difficult question: Is God silent when we suffer?

Set in 1638, the story follows a young Portuguese priest by the name of Sebastian Rodrigues, who left Rome to serve the church in the violently anti-Christian Japan of that era. Christians on the island nation were under relentless persecution. Missionaries had been banned altogether, and any who remained were captured and tortured. Rodrigues' mission was to serve as an underground missionary, and more importantly, to atone for the embarrassing apostasy of his predecessor, Father Ferreira, who under intense persecution had renounced his faith.

Father Rodrigues spent his first months in hiding, trying to make connections with local Christians in hiding. From a distance, he watched with horror as Christians were rounded up in villages and marched to their deaths. Dozens were strapped to pylons in the ocean during low tide. Then, as the evening surge rose, their cries for help became silenced by the relentless tide. In Nagasaki thousands of Christians were marched up Mount Unzen and thrown live into the molten volcano.

After just a short time in hiding, Rodrigues was caught and imprisoned by the Japanese authorities. Their demand was simple: Renounce your faith and you will be free.

The Japanese had established a system for exposing Christians. The authorities would corral all the inhabitants of a village, then set on the ground before them a *fumie* (Japanese, meaning "step-on picture"). A fumie was a plaque of wood or metal on which the image of Jesus Christ was carved or shaped.

The fumie was thrown on the ground, and a procession of villagers would line up to trample on it, a declaration that they were not of the Christian faith. The unbelievers would stomp with conviction on the fumie and often spit on it to leave no doubt in the minds of the authorities that they wanted no part of this faith. However, when Christians reached the fumie, they would refuse to trample. Their fate was clear: imprisonment, or worse, execution. One young girl dropped to her knees, gingerly picked up the fumie, wiped the dirt and spit clean with her dress, then tenderly kissed the image of the Christ. It was both a kiss of love and kiss of death.

The authorities coaxed and pleaded with Rodrigues, now imprisoned with thousands of other Christians, to trample on the fumie. Each day Christians were brought into the courtyard and shoved to their knees. If one of them refused to renounce the faith, the executioner would sprint across the courtyard and, with a swift strike of his samurai sword, behead the kneeling Christian.

The pleas from the magistrate's officials were velvety. "Put your foot on it lightly; you don't even have to really mean it," they whispered. "Just step on it once, and you will immediately be released, and the executions will end."[1]

After weeks of this agony, Rodrigues' faith began to melt.

> Stop! Stop! Lord, it is now that you should break the
> silence. You must not remain silent. Prove that you
> are justice, that you are goodness, that you are love.

You must say something to show the world that you
are the august one.… God had been silent. When the
misty rain floated over the sea, he was silent. When
the one-eyed man had been killed beneath the blazing
rays of the sun, he had said nothing.… Why is God
continually silent while those groaning voices go on? [2]

Despite his pleas to God, the torture and executions continued.
Rodrigues gave up hope, he gave up on faith, and he gave in to fear.

The priest raises his foot. In it he feels a dull, heavy
pain. This is no mere formality. He will now trample
on what he has considered the most beautiful thing
in his life, on what he has believed most pure, on
what is filled with the ideals and the dreams of man.
How his foot aches!

And then the Christ in bronze speaks to the
priest: "Trample! Trample!…"

The priest placed his foot on the *fumie*. Dawn
broke. And far in the distance the cock crew. [3]

MYSTERY AND PARADOX

Pain puts us in that place, doesn't it? We doubt God, we lose hope,
we lose trust, we lose faith. We want God to say "enough." Yet He
chooses silence. We don't like the silence at all.

Anger sets in. We demand answers. We search for explanations, no matter how elusive. We all want someone to be held accountable. And when we cannot find a person to blame, we blame God—for His apparent silence, if nothing else.

It is precisely because of God's apparent silence, as Father Rodrigues experienced, that people question God's presence in the midst of suffering. For centuries theologians and philosophers have debated what is termed *the problem of evil*. C. S. Lewis explains the quandary like this: "If God were good, he would wish to make his creatures perfectly happy, and if God were almighty he would be able to do what he wished. But the creatures are not happy. Therefore God lacks either goodness, or power, or both."[4] But this is not the conclusion of the matter. Both God and the understanding of suffering are far more complex than this simple deduction.

I prefer Christian philosopher Alvin Plantinga's answer to this question:

> Now God can create free creatures, but He can't *cause* or *determine* them to do only what is right. For if He does so, then they aren't significantly free after all; they do not do what is right *freely*. To create creatures capable of *moral good*, therefore, He must create creatures capable of moral evil; and He can't give these creatures the freedom to perform evil and at the same time prevent them from doing so.[5] Without a true freedom of choice the greatest good is not possible. God's greatest love

and good cannot be realized in a world without choice: "God did not create evil, but God created a definition of good that seems to include evil."[6]

My problem with most of the Christian answers to suffering is that they are trite. We say really shallow things about very deep problems.

In seventh grade my classmate Eric's high-school-aged brother went out to the woods behind their Mississippi home and blew his head open with a shotgun. I don't think the English language has words that would ever calm Eric's soul. You can't even try.

Eric came back to our Christian school a week after his brother's death. We were told not to talk to Eric about his brother. I guess that's how we best handle tragedy—act like nothing happened. I wanted to tell Eric I was crying on the inside. I felt so incredibly bad for him. But I never said a word. I still wish I had. Our homeroom teacher asked me to open in prayer that day. In spite of the warning to be silent, I prayed for Eric and his family. My words felt hollow. God seemed silent.

It would be naive for me to believe that I am able to provide a comprehensive or conclusive answer to the problem of pain. I just can't. On this side of heaven, I don't know that any of us will ever have a complete answer. But what I can do is explain, to a degree, why pain is necessary and why God allows His people to suffer. I can tell you with full conviction that He is always with you and never absent.

God's relationship to pain is mysterious.

People hate hearing that we can't adequately explain why bad things happen. We don't like the fact that we cannot reason out this mystery of pain.

In writing on suffering, Richard Rohr has said, "One major reason the scriptures have been so distorted and increasingly so in the last five hundred years, is because most European and North American minds have become so entirely left brain (analytical) that they cannot deal with paradox. They can't deal with both-and."[7] We struggle to make sense out of God and suffering, but we are unable. This disturbs us. But God is good, and God has allowed suffering in the world He created and controls. This is a mystery we will never fully understand.

The problem also lies in the fact that most Westerners don't like mystery. In our analytical, empirical world we want a detailed, fully comprehensible explanation of everything in life. To say there are some things in Scripture we'll never understand is deemed unacceptable. And so theologians, Christian psychiatrists, and Christian philosophers attempt to explain away the mysterious aspects of pain.

Many don't have a problem with pain as long as it afflicts those who are evil. If a murderer is shot while fleeing the police, we say, "Fine. He got what he deserved." But when tragedy strikes the innocent, the good, and the faithful, then we struggle. We want to know who is responsible. Better yet, we want someone to blame.

SILENT SCREAM

Marcus Solo was a sixth grader and one of my closest friends on the jungle mission station I grew up on in Liberia. One afternoon he came to my mother, the school nurse, to ask her to dress a machete wound that for months had festered and wouldn't heal. Her diagnosis was confirmed by doctors: Marcus had leprosy.

As Marcus left for the leprosarium, I knew it would be years before we would see him again. My twin brother and I loaded him with Danny Orlis books and board games for his quarantine.

Two months later, however, Marcus was back! The doctors gave him a letter of release, indicating that due to his early diagnosis, he could remain in boarding school. I was thrilled to have him back … but now I had a friend with leprosy! To be honest, even at the age of twelve, it was a little unnerving—because even at that age, I knew that no one really knew how contagious the disease was or how exactly it was transmitted.

We still played soccer and Monopoly daily, but I was always aware of Marcus's disease. And then one afternoon he grabbed the sunglasses off my face and put them on.

"Marcus, those are yours, dude. Keep 'em," I said, being totally honest.

One morning in church, I was sitting there minding my own business when Marcus wet his finger in his mouth and jammed it in my ear, giving me a *wet willy.*

"Dang, Marcus," I said, rubbing my ear dry. "Don't do that, my ear's gonna fall off now!"

For years I checked that ear to make sure it still had feeling and wasn't coming off.

Leprosy's greatest curse is that it robs a person of the sensation of pain. Life without pain is horrifying. Dr. Paul Brand, who spent decades in India treating leprosy victims, explains that he found painlessness to be the single most destructive aspect of the disease.[8]

For centuries physicians blamed lepers' loss of fingers, lips, and toes on *bad flesh.* Yet Brand, through his research, found that the only thing wrong with lepers' flesh was they could feel no pain. And because they had no feeling, they repeatedly caused self-inflicted wounds. "Working with patients [with leprosy] triggered the revolution in my thinking about pain. I had long recognized its value in informing injury after the fact, but I had no real appreciation for the many loyal ways in which pain protects *in advance*."[9] For example, if you and I grab the scalding handle of a pan on the stove, our nerve endings will cause a pain reflex reaction that will jerk the hand away before any damage is done. A leper will have no such reaction and will hold on tightly to the scalding handle, severely burning his hand.

One day Dr. Brand was unable to push open a door he thought was stuck shut when a small Indian boy with leprosy came up, jammed his finger into the keyhole and twisted it until the lock turned. Smiling proudly, he opened the door and pulled his bleeding finger out of the keyhole. He had cut it grossly to the bone, but he felt no more pain than if he had used the same finger to turn the page of a book.[10]

Another significant problem Brand's patients faced in India was rats. Because the patients had no reflex sensation, rats would crawl up on their beds at night and gnaw on their toes and fingers. After the problem was discovered, no patient left the leprosarium without the gift of a cat!

Many of the ulcers Dr. Brand's patients suffered came from walking on wounded feet. An ill-fitting pair of shoes would rub undetected on a toe for days. You and I would either limp or get rid of the shoes. Yet because lepers feel nothing, they continue to put full weight on the foot, making the damage worse. One patient wore a pair of shoes for months with a nail wedged in the bottom that tore his heel to shreds, yet he kept wearing the shoes. The more the patients began to understand the disease, the more they dreaded life without pain. Ironically, they began to wish for pain. One patient, Raman, who repeatedly injured himself unknowingly, finally asked, "Dr. Brand, how can I ever be free without pain?"[11]

Similarly, perhaps pain is good for the soul. Without knowing what is painful, we may never know what is beautiful.

HE WHISPERS IN THE SILENCE

Most of us are not comfortable with silence. Did you ever sit across the table from a college date when the conversation went stone cold? You couldn't think of one solitary thing to say! The silence was killing you. All you could hear were the crickets. You just wanted to crawl under the table.

Silence is foreign to American culture. We are a loud people. Travel to any city outside the United States and sit by a hotel pool. I'll point out all the Americans in five minutes. We fill our lives with noise and things that make noise. But noise is draining and saps the soul. You will never become a deep person in the noise. God speaks in the silence.

I've stood at the top of Mount Sinai, where Elijah waited to hear God. Elijah said God wasn't in the ferocious wind, He wasn't in the violent earthquake, He wasn't in the blazing fire … rather, He whispered in the silence.[12]

When you hit a place in life when you hear nothing else, it's then that you will hear God. Get out of the noise and the traffic and find a place of solace where God can speak. If life's pain seems unbearable today, then stop and listen. He wants to speak—but He won't shout.

HE'S WITH YOU IN THE SILENCE

One of my favorite attributes of God is that He is the I-Am-with-you God. In spite of the fact that we cannot adequately understand why pain exists, we can know with great certainty that God is with us.

Never will I leave you; never will I forsake you. [13]

We are also not alone in our suffering, since Christ has gone before us. He lived in this world and endured the worst pain this world can inflict: "For we do not have a high priest who is unable to sympathize with our weaknesses."[14] Scottish theologian Horatius Bonar has said, "Jesus weeps with us. 'In all our affliction he is afflicted.' He knows our sorrows, for he has passed through them all, and therefore he feels for us. He is touched with the feeling of our griefs as well as our infirmities."[15] John Stott has also written, "The God who allows us to suffer, once suffered himself in Christ, and continues to suffer with us and for us today.… The cross of Christ is the proof of God's … personal, loving solidarity with us in our pain."[16]

Philip Yancey asks, "Where is God when it hurts?" in his book by the same title. Answer: "He has been there from the beginning.… He has joined us. He has hurt and bled and cried and suffered. He has dignified for all time those who suffer, by sharing their pain."[17]

In the final book of the Bible, we read there was silence in heaven.

If in heaven, God is in the silence—

He must also be present in the
silence on earth.

ON THE INSIDE

I cry on the inside where no one can hear or see.
Wishing there's someone out there that
   actually understands me.
I scream no one hears me.
I cry on the inside where no one can hear or see.
Has no one told you she's not okay?
She's dying on the inside.
hurting on the out.
Suffering in silence.
Trying to find a way out.
Figuring out who she wants to be.
I cry on the inside where no one can hear or see.[18]

Sabrina Correll

Scott Erickson

PART II

GRAY DAYS

Clouds and thick darkness are all around him.
Psalm 97:2¹

Rainy days and Mondays—and gray days—get everybody down.

Life without Christ would be like living in a gray-colored world.

It would kind of be like living in Seattle, Chicago, or Oregon. I used to live outside Chicago, and the first winter about did me in. The cold was unbearable, but the gray days suck the life right out of your soul. The newscasters count the consecutive days with no sunshine. At one point they hit "thirty straight days with no sunshine!"; they think it's funny, some kind of odd Midwestern humor.

I've been to Oregon too. I took my family there on our summer vacation, and we stayed with my sister for a week. It rained every day, all day. Not a hard rain, not a downpour—just a drizzle. Just enough to drive you mad, like Chinese water torture.

I think the gray days in Oregon make people want to give up on life. I saw grown men wear bedroom slippers to the grocery store. I saw people headed to work in sweats. Life-coach advice: If you show up to work in sweats, you've just told everyone that you give up. You'll never get a promotion, you'll never get a raise, no one will ever call you *sir* or *ma'am*. That's it.

By the end of the week in Oregon, we had all succumbed. All that my kids wanted to do was sit on the couch under a Snuggie and sip hot cocoa. That's not good.

Life gets like that sometimes.

For you, maybe life isn't dark. Maybe it's just gray.

The dark days are when we're punched in the gut so hard we can hardly breathe. Gray days suck the life out of us in a different way. On life's gray days we catatonically exist with the lost dream, the constant disappointment, the repeated failure.

The religious rulers of Jesus' day tried to keep the sky gray. On the second day, the day after the crucifixion, the day before the resurrection, they went to Pilate and said, "We remember that while he was still alive that deceiver said, 'After three days I will rise again.' So give the order for the tomb to be made secure until the third day."[2]

On the second day, when the skies turned gray, Pilate stationed guards at the tomb to keep the Christ in a stone cave. On the gray days of life, we want to give up. We stop believing.

The second day looked hopeless.

The gray days feel hopeless.

But actually, it's a pretty funny thought: *Let's keep God in a stone-gray cave!*

You can't.

GARDEN ON THE MOON

My dad was turning eighty and said he wanted to climb Mount Sinai because Moses climbed the same mountain when he was eighty. (Kinda crazy, but I liked his thinking.) So he flew my wife and me and five of my brothers and sisters and in-laws to Egypt's Sinai Peninsula.

On the early-morning drive from our hotel (in Sharm el-Sheikh, on the stunning coral banks of the Red Sea) to Mount Sinai, all I could think about was, *How in the world did the Hebrew people live in this God-forsaken desert for forty years?* For three hours all we saw were rocks and dirt. It looked like the moon. If you're a conspiracy theorist and question the moon landing, I'll tell you right where they filmed it (not that I don't think you're nuts): on the Sinai Peninsula.

At the base of Mount Sinai sits the fifteen-hundred-year-old St. Catherine's monastery. I had heard that they claim to have built the monastery around Moses' burning bush. Before driving through the Sinai desert, I had mocked the notion—"How could they ever know that's the right bush?!"

When our van dropped us off at the base of Mount Sinai, we poked our heads in the monastery to take a look at "Moses' burning bush" (it's actually a tree), and I thought, "Hmm, they may have something here—this is the only living plant within two hundred miles!"

My dad did great climbing the mountain. As we neared the summit, we came to a small plateau, a basin in the mountain about five hundred feet below the peak. A sign pointed toward it that read *Elijah's Garden.* And that's what it is. In the middle of the moon is a garden. Honestly. I couldn't believe it. Trees, green grass, plants, bushes with flowers. I have no idea how it got there or how things grow there, but they do.

The Bible says Elijah lived there.[3] When life got nasty and he was discouraged and he felt like he couldn't take it any more, God led him to this garden in the rocks, a garden that looks like it just dropped right out of the sky, straight down from heaven.

Maybe it did.

All of us want to find the garden in the desert, the hope in the pain, but it's not that easy. It doesn't come that quickly. It's not right there. Sometimes God lets us live in the gray days for a long time.

Maybe you're there right now. We get by, we survive. We exist. Life becomes a rut and a tired routine. We've lost our dreams and desires. We've given up on doing anything great with our lives.

If someone were to ask, "What happened?" we'd say, "Life turned gray."

Chapter 5

DIRTY LITTLE SECRETS

"Your Father ... sees what is done in secret."
Matthew 6:4

"You called me an idiot, so I sent your bags to the wrong city. Oops! I guess you were right."

That's one of the thousands of messages sent to Frank Warren since he invited people from everywhere to anonymously share their deepest, darkest secrets. Frank says he has been floored by the response. He had no idea people were dying to get the weight of a secret off their chests.

"You stole the theme for my wedding ... so now my theme will be: Everything better than YOUR wedding!"

"If my mother-in-law mentions the muffins
at Costco one more time, I'm going to burn the
place down."

What surprised Frank the most, he says, is that people turned
their secrets into art. As the secrets poured in, people did not simply
write their words of confession on a blank piece of paper; they put
them on photographs, cut them out of newspaper print, colored
them with drawings and images of their secrets and secret pain. Their
hearts were spilling out with their words.

Secrets get serious.

"I tell everyone that my father died in Iraq. But
in reality, he killed himself when he got back."

"I didn't realize what a good husband he
was—until I left and joined a divorce support
group. Error. Error. Error."

"I trashed my parents' house to look like I
had a party while they were out of town … so
my mom would think I had friends."

"Sometimes I lie about the time in the
morning, so she'll stay next to me a little
longer."

"My mom chose my stepdad over me."

"I'm tired of taking pills to make me feel better."[1]

The world we live in is full of secrets. Presidents hide secrets about interns; investment bankers have secret ways of handling money; governors have secret ambitions to be senators; baseball players have secrets about their home runs; NBA referees make secret deals with bookies; politicians hide secrets that hurt their wives.

Our secrets are our shame: addictions, dishonesty, unfaithfulness, abuse, financial problems.

Secrets turn us dark on the inside. That's the problem with secrets.

Arguably the most famous secret (that's an oxymoron for you) in the Bible involved King David and his secrets with Bathsheba. Theirs is a story of sex and lies and secrets.

Secrets often begin when you find yourself somewhere you shouldn't be. This line in the Bible tells us where trouble starts: "At the time when kings go off to war ... David remained in Jerusalem."[2]

David was somewhere he had no business being. He was supposed to be at work. He was supposed to be doing the business of leading a nation. Instead he was at home, on the couch watching SportsCenter, sipping a Diet Coke. He was bored and aimless and ripe for temptation.

When you land yourself in a place you have no business being, you're inviting trouble. If David had been where he belonged, we would have never heard Bathsheba's name.

Then we read, "He saw a woman bathing. The woman was very beautiful...."[3] Okay, he just flipped the channel from ESPN to Pay-Per-View. And he stayed, and watched, and lingered, and lusted, and fixated, and refused to change the channel.

Can I tell you what the Bible teaches about temptation? RUN. Get away from it. Don't go near it. The writers of the Bible were brilliant. When men are sexually aroused, a chemical reaction literally happens in the body. There's a chemistry to sensuality. Run.

In his book *Temptation*, Dietrich Bonhoeffer writes, "Satan does not ... fill us with hatred for God, but with forgetfulness of God.... Therefore the Bible teaches us in times of temptation in the flesh, there is one command: Flee! Flee! ... There is no resistance to Satan in lust other than flight."[4]

I'm proud of my friend Blair. He does this. Blair was on a business road trip with several colleagues from his office. After dinner he headed to his room for the night. As he got ready for bed, there was a knock at the hotel-room door. He opened it to see one of his colleagues standing in front of him, wearing a seductive smile, tiny shorts, a cut-off T-shirt, a bottle of wine in one hand, and two wine glasses in the other. She said to him, "You want to watch some porn?"

Yikes.

Blair said he thanked her for the offer but said, "No, I can't." And shut the door.

When Blair reported this to our small group, I said, "Wow, Blair! That's impressive. You are either the strongest man I know … or that was one butt-ugly woman!"

Run. Run like the wind. Run like Joseph from Potiphar's wife. Run like Blair. If you don't turn and shut the door, close the window, turn off the TV, and run—it's just a matter of time. If you linger, you will be sucked in.

THE DIRT ON SECRETS

Here are a few truths about secrets:

Little Secrets Become Big Obsessions

Secret desires turn into secret actions that grow a life of their own.

David's acquaintances see what's happening and try to warn him: "Is this not Bathsheba, the daughter of Eliam, the *wife* of Uriah the Hittite?"[5] He uses the "w" word! Wife! Bomb on an airplane!

The problem is our secrets become our obsessions.

Tolstoy tells about the time his older brother told him to stand in the corner and not think about the fact that a huge white bear was coming down the hallway toward him. But he said the more he tried *not* to think about the bear, the more he thought about the bear. The bear filled his mind.

Our minds have this odd way of connecting everything around us to our secrets. Researchers say that when a person sits in a room and tries to forget a secret, all the items in the room one by one connect themselves to the secret—the fan, the coffee table, the lamp, the dog. The "tiny" secret grows to become our greatest obsession.

David is obsessed. In spite of the warnings and red flags, "David sent messengers to get her. She came to him, and he slept with her."[6]

Hidden Secrets Create Public Problems

Then we read, "[Bathsheba] conceived and sent word to David, saying, 'I am pregnant.'"[7] Houston, we've got a problem.

A secret never tells the whole truth about itself ... sin is a liar!

Secrets never tell you, "I can't be hidden. I'll wreck your family. I'll ruin your reputation. I'll cost you your job. I'll drain your bank account. I'll cause you years of heartache and regret ... this is the beginning of a long, sorrowful, dead-end road."

Secret desires cause us to sacrifice the permanent for the temporary. We lose all sight of what is important to satisfy an immediate desire.

Secrets Multiply and Reproduce

Like cells regenerate, secrets multiply and reproduce.

When David tried to bury his secret, he amplified it instead. It's like trying to stuff a bobcat in your lunch pail ... it will go berserk.

David had two choices here: (a) stop the lying and come clean or (b) create more secrets and multiply the problem.

He chose (b): "Send me Uriah the Hittite."[8] Not a good plan. Uriah was Bathsheba's husband. Uriah was the man David wasn't; he was the warrior David used to be. He had integrity.

So David stoops lower and has him killed.

But now people are talking. The prophet Samuel arrives and tells David a story about a rich man who takes advantage of a poor man. David is vexed. Then Samuel cuts him with words: "You are the man!"[9]

Busted! The cat's out of the bag. Game over.

Our secrets have a strange way of finding us out.

Like Jonah in the Bible, we think we can con God.

That's childish thinking. Joan Peskin, a professor of psychology at the University of Toronto, writes about her three-year-old son, who often climbed up on the cabinet when she was out of the kitchen to swipe a cookie. One afternoon, when the smell of freshly baked chocolate chips filled the house, he anxiously walked in and out of the kitchen. Finally, out of frustration, thinking his mother might never leave the kitchen, Joan's three-year-old blurted out, "Mom, get out of the kitchen—I want to get a cookie."

You're not three years old. You know God sees you. You have nothing to hide, so come clean.

This reality finally hits David, so he writes, "O Lord, you have searched me and you know me. You know when I sit and when I rise; you perceive my thoughts from afar. You discern my going out and my lying down; you are familiar with all my ways."[10]

Secrets Muddy Life Inside and Out

When David finally comes clean, he blurts out, "God, I've got dirt inside!"[11]

Here's the bottom line: Secrets will muddy your life inside and out. Secrets affect us physically. People with secrets are far more likely to have health problems. For example, Harvard researcher Anita Kelly has found that women with breast cancer who have no secrets live twice as long as those who carry secrets.[12]

Secrets have this way of making us feel dirty on the inside.

Our culture realizes this so we use language like "I have dirt on him," "He has a dirty mind," "She's got a dirty mouth," "He has dirty thoughts," "That's a dirty movie." One network even aired a show titled "Dirt," about dirty things.

If you've ever carried a secret, you feel like mud on the inside. And when we feel dirty, we feel shame. Shame is the outcome, the result, the offspring of secrets.

Shame is not guilt; it's different. Shame connects what happened to who you are. Guilt, for example, says, "I did something bad." Shame says, "I am bad." Shame runs deep. Guilt says, "I don't like what I did." Shame says, "I don't like who I am." Shame says things like, "I am worthless, a failure.... I am dirty."

But I'm here to say you don't have to live full of dirt and shame and secrets anymore.

You are not dirt. Christ has made you clean.

COME CLEAN

"Wash me!" David finally pleads.[13]

Princeton theologian Frederick Buechner says, "To confess your sins to God is not to tell him anything he doesn't already know. Until you confess them, however, they are the abyss between you. When you confess them, they become the bridge."[14]

Bottled-up secrets make your chest feel like it's about to explode.

But when you come clean, you breathe this great sigh of relief—"It's out, it's over, I can stop acting, I can stop pretending, I can stop the lies."

William Young, the author of *The Shack*, says, "When I became honest about my trouble, my reputation went out the window, but I became the freest man in the world."[15]

The lie Satan wants you to swallow is, *You are what you did.* Or, *You are what someone did to you.* Or, *You are dirty; you are ugly.*

The truth Christ wants you to realize is, *You are not what you did. You are not what someone did to you. You are who God says you are—clean and beautiful, like a bride on her wedding day.*

Your life of secrets can end right here, today, right now.

THROUGH SHADES OF GRAY

These times to me bring agony—
I'm not the girl I want to be.
I wish that everyone could see—
I'm so much more than agony.

And even though it seems so dark—
I dream of sunshine in the park.
I wish for the clouds to part—
But I still see shadows in my heart.

And soon through shades of gray—
I hope good memories will show and stay.
I'll dream once more of a better day—
And saunter on along my way.

For if the clouds keep rolling in—
I fear my patience will wear thin.
My heart will falter, sink in sin—
My mind may suddenly give in.[16]

Chapter 6

FEAR LOCKER

There is no fear in love.
1 John 4:18

Fear is where God meets you. Fear is when you need Him most. Fear is when you become alive to His presence.

The rain was steady, as it always is in the late afternoon during rainy season. The sky darkened from gray to black as we sat on our front porch, watching daylight slip into a dark African night—when suddenly an enormous bolt of lightning crashed through the ominous canopy and slammed into the jungle below.

My first seven years growing up in Africa, we lived deep in the Liberian jungle. For hundreds of miles, there was nothing but the world's thickest rain forest. The only way into our jungle mission station was on a single-engine Cessna 180 airplane.

As a kid there was plenty to be afraid of. Snakes were everywhere—spitting cobras, gaboon vipers, and green mambas (also known as the five-step mamba—once bitten you're dead in five steps). Occasionally we would find them in our house. The jungle was also filled with army ants. Every few months several million would invade our house, usually at night, and I would wake up covered in ants all trying to get a chunk of my skin. Then there were the bush devils, who struck fear in every kid. They were guys wearing evil masks and grass skirts who would show up dancing wildly to the music of their drum-beating, machete-wielding posse. We would run like we had stolen something when we saw them coming. My Liberian friends also had me petrified of the *genah*. These were supposedly little short men who lived in the mountains and had evil powers. I never saw one, but I wasn't foolish enough to climb the surrounding hills to look for them either. There were also the Heartmen, dressed all in white and carrying a gunnysack. The Heartmen would wander the back alleys of cities or hide on jungle trails and kidnap kids for use in ritualistic sacrifices. This really happened! But none of these fears rocked my heart like lightning.

Most of us tend to be rather ambivalent about lightning. But when a thunderstorm rolls in over the jungle in Africa, it wreaks havoc. When I was twelve, we endured a rainy season I'll never forget. First, my pet chimp was hit. A bolt slammed into the giant tree she was chained to, came down the trunk and up the chain, and lit her up. The next day she sat under her tree and began wiggling her teeth out one at a time, until they were all gone. Since she ate only bananas, we supposed it could have been worse.

Now, just a week later, we watched this tremendous bolt slam into the trees just a few hundred yards away. Seconds later we heard screaming. Then a young student came sprinting up to our house. "Where's Reverend Chinchen?" he shouted anxiously. "Mary German and Elizabeth have been hit by lightning!"

My father jumped into his jeep and raced to where the two girls lay under the large cottonwood tree. They had taken off their flip-flops, thrown them into the metal buckets on their heads, and run for cover from the rain under the tree. And the tree pulled the lightning bolt right down on top of them.

They smelled like burnt flesh. My dad tried mouth-to-mouth resuscitation, but he knew it was pointless.

Mary German was dead.

I remember standing outside the wake the next night and hearing a strange mix of wailing and thumping music. I wanted to be anywhere but there. I didn't want to be in the jungle. I didn't want to be in Africa. I was full of fear.

My kids make me check under the bed and close the closet door before I leave their rooms at night; they don't like the dark. But even when we grow up, we don't particularly like the dark.

We don't like the feeling of being afraid, but fear is often where we meet God. Fear makes our senses come alive to His presence. In many ways we are most alive when we are afraid. You know what I mean if you've been there.

The moment fear hits, your body reacts. Your stomach turns. Your heart beats madly. Adrenaline floods your veins. Your chest tightens. You feel dizzy and light-headed. You have difficulty breathing. You perspire and sweat. Your mind races … and surprisingly, you see everything more clearly. Your hearing sharpens, your eyes focus, your strength increases.

All people wrestle with fear. On some days it's stronger than others. And when it is, we usually tap out, and fear dominates our lives.

> We fear being evaluated—and criticized—at work.
> We fear taxes. We fear death. Sometimes taxes more than death!
> We fear judgment from God.
> We fear failure.
> We fear for the safety of our kids.
> We fear disease.
> We fear change and the unknown.
> We fear the disapproval of others.
> We fear bills at the end of the month.
> We fear cancer and heart attacks.
> We fear crime.
> We fear speaking in public.
> We fear the first day of junior high.
> We fear confrontation.

We fear heights, close places, spiders, and public restrooms. Life gives us plenty to fear.

Fear keeps God's people trapped in a locker. Fear keeps us far from God. Fear is why the disciples followed at a distance. Fear is why Peter said three times he didn't know Jesus. The cock crowed. He chickened out. Fear is why Moses wandered for forty years. Fear is why Abraham lied about Sarah being his wife. Fear is why Jonah ran.

Fear keeps us living in the gray days.

THE PROBLEM OF FEAR

Have you ever wondered why it's always the nineteen-year-olds who are bungee jumping, sky surfing, white-water rafting, glacier climbing, extreme skiing, and fire walking? Have you wondered why boys, when they attempt to jump from the roof of your house into your swimming pool and miss, simply think it was bad luck and try again? It's because the phrase *NO FEAR* is not simply a T-shirt slogan; it's a way of life.

Fear does a strange thing to the human mind; it convinces us we are failures. A region of the brain called the amygdala remembers bad experiences and tells us to be afraid. When we are young, this space is largely void, giving us little reason to fear failure. But as we age, this region fills with memories of past failures and causes us to instinctively behave more cautiously and become more concerned with failure. At the same time, to the extent our amygdala fills up with reasons to fear, our faith diminishes. This is the reason why all golfers, as they age, become horrible putters. The yips set in.

Christians everywhere face this great dilemma of fear and faith. We want to live lives of fantastic faith, but reality always stares us in the face. Naysayers speak up, so we slow down, hesitate, and are stopped in our tracks by fear. Fear is a serious impediment to faith.

Fear causes us to move as if we are in a bad dream—very slowly. We want to run, but our legs are rubber. That's the problem of fear. Fear slows us down and disallows God from using our lives effectively. I know fear has kept great people off the mission field. I have seen fear of failure keep students out of college. I have watched fear keep a person from pursuing a more challenging career. Fear will ruin your future and melt your faith.

A close friend of mine was considering moving to Africa to serve as a medical missionary doctor. My father, a thirty-eight-year veteran missionary to Africa, had been communicating with him, encouraging him, and telling him how great the need is there. When it looked like this young doctor would be making the decision to go, his father called my father. His words were surprising, particularly coming from a man my father knew well—a Christian, a medical doctor himself, and even a church elder. He called to say, "Jack, would you quit telling my son to move to Africa?"

"Why do you say that?" my father asked.

"Because Jim [not his actual name] could die there," he retorted. "What if he is in a car accident and his legs are completely severed—where would he be treated?"

There are always naysayers, the voices of the prophets of doom: "Don't try it. It's too dangerous. You'll get sick. You'll lose your job.

It's too difficult for you." Instead, listen to the voice of God whispering in your ear: "I need you. I will take care of you. I will empower you. I will change you."

Jim listened to God's voice. He's served in Africa with his wife and children for almost ten years now, fearlessly treating people with AIDS, malaria, yellow fever, and bilharzia.

Fear constricts the human soul and locks us up in a cage of uncertainty. Fear makes us live in a thick fog. Once fear settles in the heart, it causes us to be afraid of practically everything in life: a noise in the dark, a trip to the store. The person struggling with fear lives in a world filled with *what ifs*: What if I have an accident? What if the food makes me sick? What if I fail? What if he disappoints me? As Brennan Manning says, "Once these questions guide our lives, we take out a second mortgage in the house of fear."[1] Or to put it another way, when these questions dominate our lives, it becomes impossible to live from a place of faith.

THE GOOD IN FEAR

Fear is an instrument God often uses to turn people to Him. God uses fear to test resolve. God uses fear to force us to depend on Him alone.

Live Full of Faith

In John Ortberg's excellent book on faith, *If You Want to Walk on Water, You've Got to Get Out of the Boat*, he reminds us that the command to "fear not" is the most-often-repeated challenge in the Bible. On 366 occasions God reminds His people to stop trembling and start living. "I think God says 'fear not' so often because fear is the number one reason human beings are tempted to avoid doing what God asks them to do."[2]

Fear is the price of great faith. Every person of great faith faced fear. But what sets people of faith apart is their willingness to move ahead despite fear. And maybe the fear will never go away, but we can trust God to carry us through.

A friend of mine, Bret, who spent eight years planting a church in Las Vegas, calls the fear pastors experience *spiritual nausea.* I've spent time in the church-planting business myself, and I know exactly what he's talking about.

But just because you feel fear in whatever you attempt for God, that doesn't mean you should quit or turn back or not do it—in fact, maybe it's just the opposite. I think it's in our moments of desperate fear that God is at His best. Steven Pressfield says it brilliantly: "Fear is an indicator of what you *must* do."[3]

Bret tells of a morning about one year into their church plant when he called his staff together. Giving had not improved, they had piles of bills to pay, and there would be little left for payroll. So he gathered his staff to tell them they would all need to go out and find second jobs, at Starbucks or wherever. As he began sharing the discouraging news, one of the girls around the table who was opening the mail handed Bret a $15,000 check from an envelope she had just opened. "Praise God!" Bret exclaimed, "Get back to work; we're still in business."

He Really Is in Control

Central to Christian theology is the idea that God is sovereign; in other words, He is in ultimate control. Nothing happens, or happens to you, outside of His will.

This piece of doctrine is packed with hope and promise for the Christ follower because it explains that someone much greater and more powerful than you and me has His hand on our lives. Tragedy is not outside God's realm of control; nothing happens outside His plan for your life … and it's a wonderful one.

I love a great roller coaster, and I've ridden my share. My hands-down favorite is the Xcelerator at Knott's in Southern California. The explosive start shoots you out of the platform to eighty-two miles per hour in 2.3 seconds. Your head snaps back, and the g-force kicks in. Within seconds you're launched up a 205-foot ascent only to drop straight down, literally, over the other side.

Maybe we place too much trust in the engineers. But because we know the roller coaster is well designed, soundly constructed, and safety tested, we trust it. The entire experience is exhilarating. We scream, we want to spew, and then when we realize we'll live, we can laugh.

In many ways, life is like that. We have a Designer who has a perfect path for our life, and we need to trust just a little more that He will carry us through. We have the thrilling moments when we think, "Wow, life is amazing." Then we have the out-of-control day. We have the dips and the down days. We have the days when we feel like the bottom has fallen out of life. But hold on, fear not, know that the One who has engineered the universe has a wonderful, thrilling plan for your life. The Old Testament prophet Jeremiah reminds us of this: "'I know the plans I have for you,' declares the LORD, 'plans to prosper you and not to harm you, plans to give you hope and a future.'"[4]

I AM with You

One of the great promises of the Bible is that God will be with you. He promised this to Abraham, Moses, Joshua, and Gideon. This was Jesus' promise to His closest followers: "I will beg the Father, and he will give you another Comforter."[5] And His own name, Immanuel, reminds us of this truth—God with us.

A few summers back I was in a bike rental shop in Tahoe, and they had a video running of guys bungee jumping off a bridge. Intrigued, I stopped to watch. "Why are two guys strapped together?" I asked the pierced and tattooed store employee who was watching with me and trying to get me to sign up for a jump.

"He's the instructor," he answered.

Instructor? I thought. *Once you leap off the bridge with your life suspended by a rubber band, what good in the world will an instructor do?*

The two sailed off the bridge headfirst, bound at the ankles. Hurtling toward the water, the bungee cord stretched … but did not stop their fall. With a crack and a splash, they both slammed in the river below before being yanked back up.

"Were they supposed to do that?" I asked tat guy.

"No, the guy in front got a concussion. But, dude, wasn't that rad? Hey, you ready to sign up for a jump?"

Oh, could I, I thought, *and would you let me have that highly skilled instructor?*

This might be a simple example, but a bungee instructor strapped to your back is useless. However, God with you is an entirely different matter. His presence changes everything.

Sara Groves is a talented and well-known Christian musician, but she is maybe best known for her passion for hurting women. Sara has become involved with International Justice Mission (IJM) and tells the story of Elizabeth.

Elizabeth grew up in Southeast Asia with a love for God. At fifteen she left home for boarding school. The family friend who was traveling with her betrayed the family and allowed her to be kidnapped in exchange for money. The kidnappers smuggled her across the border to the neighboring country where sex slavery is rampant. There she was sold to a brothel.

For seven months Elizabeth was held prisoner in a cell and sold several times a day for sex. Yet every day she prayed and begged God to free her. The other girls in the brothel would mock her and say, "God is not here, Elizabeth. God may be out there somewhere, but God is not in this hellhole of a place."

Elizabeth kept praying and trusting that God would hear.

International Justice Mission learned of Elizabeth and the other girls held prisoner and, with the help of local police, raided the brothel at night. As they hurriedly gathered Elizabeth's few possessions, the IJM workers noticed a Bible verse Elizabeth had written on the wall above her bed.

> The Lord is my light and my salvation—whom shall
> I fear?

The LORD is the stronghold of my life—of whom
shall I be afraid?[6]

A few months after being rescued, IJM asked Elizabeth if she
would share her story. When she agreed, they asked if she would
share the verse she had written on the wall.

She said, "No, I'm sorry. I can't share that verse now. God gave
me that verse when I was a prisoner. Those were the words He spoke
to me then. But God has spoken new words to me now, and I would
be happy to share those." And so she shared words from the psalmist:

The righteous cry out, and the LORD hears them; he
delivers them from all their troubles.

The LORD is close to the brokenhearted and saves
those who are crushed in spirit.[7]

GOD REWARDS FEARLESS LIVING

Where there is fear, God can replace it with faith. While fear shows a
lack of confidence in God, a crisis is an opportunity for us to express
faith in God's sustaining power.

Just out of graduate school, my wife and I took a short teaching
assignment at a Christian college in Liberia, Africa. Less than two
years into our stay, civil war broke out in the country. Veronica was
six months pregnant with our first child, so our initial response was
to leave the country. But as we processed and prayed, I began to
wonder, "Palmer, where is your faith?"

We prayed hard and asked God to remove our apprehension. We made the decision to remain ... with some trepidation, but filled with faith that God would take care of us. He did. However, two months later, rebel forces moved even closer. As their capture of our city became imminent, and when two American missionaries were killed in an ambush just a few miles away, the college closed and the U.S. embassy gave orders for all Americans to evacuate our city.

Veronica, then eight months pregnant, and I left for the capital city of Monrovia, driving fifty miles through territory controlled by the rebels. Numerous people fleeing the area had already been killed in ambushes, so we knew it would be a dangerous drive. In broad daylight, the single-lane dirt road lay in deep shadows from the canopy of trees that choke the Liberian rain forest. The wall of jungle was close and thick, and we could not see more than a few feet into the foliage. Cresting every hill, rounding every corner, I was certain we would encounter an ambush. It felt like a dark valley in the shadow of death. As I pushed our Peugeot to ridiculous speeds down the dirt road, I considered what to do if we hit a rebel ambush. Should I blow through it at full speed, or brake hard and make a U-turn? I decided I would blow through. For more than one hour as we drove through that rebel-controlled area, not one shot was fired at us. The following day the road was permanently closed as people were killed in ambushes traveling the exact route we took.

Here's my point: God honors the steps of faith we take—even when we are full of fear. Don't ask God to remove the fear; ask Him to fill you with faith. God rewards our faith and ...

He

will

carry

you

through

the

darkest

days.

WATCH THE ANGELS FLY

We'll watch the angels fly …
Save me now before the world falls
Save me before the angel of death calls

I am a wanderer, lost in starry time
Strolling through my endless mind
My life at times seems all in vain
A mystery … arcane

So join me and watch the angels fly
Then you and I will ride the crimson sky
You saved me before the world did fall
You saved me before master death called.[8]

C. Basham

Chapter 7

THE WAR OF FOG

All night long on my bed I looked for the one my heart loves.
Song of Solomon 3:1

I was walking through our living room when my eye caught the title of an article listed on the cover of a woman's glamour magazine: *Downsize Your Things. Wow,* I thought. *That's deep, that's biblically deep. And that could preach! We all need to live that way!* I mentally retracted all the cheap shots I had taken at magazines like this that seemed to contain little more than mental cotton candy. (And I refuse to mention here who in our home reads these magazines ... but six people live in our house: me, four sons, and my wife. I'll let you do the math).

With a newfound respect for this tabloid rag, I picked it up, sat down, and turned straight to the article and started to read.

But as I read, nothing made sense. Rather confused, I flipped back to look at the title of the article and realized I had misread. It wasn't *Downsize Your Things* ... the title was actually *Downsize Your Thighs!*

Great.

All of us need to downsize the busyness of life. Hurry and busyness will fog life. Like the maddening confusion of battle that soldiers describe as *the fog of war*, life lived at such a pace—rushed, hurried, and hectic—turns into a gray fog.

BUSYNESS

There's no question that we are a busy people. We rush through busy weeks to get to busier weekends. We hurry to work. Rush our kids to school. And try to make it home before dark.

No one does one thing at a time. We multitask all day long.

The *e* world seems to have accelerated the pace. Regular mail is now referred to as snail paced. So we survive in the *e* world of now: *e*mail, *e*ticket, *e*vite, *e*card,

We end up going places and doing things only because they are fast. For example, none us go to McDonalds for the great food—you don't even go there because it's cheap food; you go there because it's *fast* food. The CEO of Domino's once made the statement, "We don't sell pizza, we sell delivery." He's right; if you can't get a pizza to my couch in thirty minutes, I want it for free!

Sherwood Lingenfelter and Marvin Mayers write about tensions over time.[1] In the South Pacific, for example, the acceptable period of lateness is about two hours. People feel tension at three hours. In Latin America the acceptable period of lateness is thirty minutes; at one hour, people feel tension. In the United States, however, the acceptable period for lateness is just five minutes—at fifteen minutes people feel anger! They'll leave Chipotle in a huff because they think you stood them up. I think it's worse in England. It's like you can be a minute late, but at five minutes they throw your tea out.

Being too busy for God has always been a problem with people. Do you remember the well-intentioned man who came to Jesus and said something like, "I will follow You wherever You go … but I've got a lot of stuff going on at home I need to take care of first"? Jesus said, "Leave it."[2] The guy wouldn't.

And of course you know Martha, who threw Mary under the bus when she didn't think Mary was busy enough: "Lord, don't you care that my sister has left me to do the work by myself? Tell her to help me!"[3]

But Jesus knew about the problem of busyness and how it robs us of intimacy with him. "Martha, Martha," the Lord answered, "you are worried and upset about many things, but only one thing is needed."[4]

Jesus knew that we skim on life when we hurry. We end up having superficial conversations, with superficial friends, in superficial lives. When you hurry, your soul turns numb. Relationships become plastic.

Most of us believe we can maintain a busy, hectic, nonstop schedule and have it not affect our relationships. That's a false assumption.

Sociologists are realizing this; they are saying *quality time* is a myth. Kids don't do meetings. You can't raise them in short, scheduled bursts. They need lots of attention. Psychologist Ronald Levant says, "Quality time is just a way of deluding ourselves into shortchanging our children.... It's an illusion to think they're going to be on your timetable, and that you can say, 'Okay, we've got a half hour, let's get on with it.'"[5]

If you give all you've got to your work, for example, there will be very little of you left when you get home. Comedian Rob Becker explains the problem like this, "Most women on average speak twelve thousand words a day. Men, on the other hand, speak on average four thousand words a day. So when we men come home at night and don't talk much, our wives often ask, 'Why aren't you saying anything? Why won't you talk to me?' What wives don't realize is that we're simply all out of words."

What children and wives need—what everyone needs—is lots of time. Or our souls turn hollow. You cannot maintain a maddening schedule and expect to deeply love your kids, or your wife, or God.

And that's one of the great problems of busyness; it leaves little time for God. If your life is a zoo, I would guess that your relationship with God is shallow. Sorry to be so blunt. But I know that wild days and weeks leave no time for prayer, meditation, worship, contemplation, introspection, or any other practice that feeds the soul: "Noise and frenzied, hectic schedules dull our senses, closing our ears to His still, small voice and making us numb to His touch."[6]

Why are we such a busy people? Maybe because we're such an entertainment-driven society. We jet our kids from swim to soccer to cheer to dance, doing all we can to keep them from being bored!

Not long ago we were on vacation in San Diego and left my eight-year-old son with a sitter, his older cousin. When we came back from dinner, she was a bit upset and told us he had created a commotion at the hotel when he dialed 911.

We sat him down and asked why in the world he had called 911. His answer was simple and matter-of-fact: "I was bored."

He's right. Boredom seems to be a crime in our country. Haha.

I also believe we are a frantic people because we equate busyness with success. Hidden in our conscience is the belief that the busier lives we live, the more important we are. Because, think about it, when people ask, "How's work?" we always say, "Busy! Crazy busy!"

No one says, "Ah, things are quiet. I really don't do much at all. I spend most of my day updating Facebook and taking naps." No. Nobody wants to be that honest.

So we try to impress people with our busyness.

Here are a few suggestions for the rushed and run-ragged:

DOWNSIZE YOUR SCHEDULE

Practice slowing. Researchers say there's no correlation between hurry and productivity. It's a false assumption that rushing will help you accomplish more. So downsize your schedule. It's okay to do less today.

Maybe try a few of these things:

- Drive in the slow lane on the freeway. It will make you nuts, but your blood pressure will drop.
- Eat more slow food, like artichokes.
- Refuse to multitask anymore. When a friend calls, don't channel surf or check your email. BTW: They can hear the keyboard clicking anyway.
- Leave your watch at home for a week.
- Take an e-holiday. Try going one week without texting, emailing, tweeting, or facebooking. I know you think your world will crash, but it may be one of the most freeing weeks you've had in years.
- Accomplish one thing a day. Okay, don't get fired. But I mean one big thing a day. Focus on that. Do it well. And fill the rest of your day with people and with God.

In the Psalms we read, "Be still, and know that I am God."[7] If you want a deep, meaningful relationship with God or with any person, you will have to slow down.

If you fail to downsize your schedule, you are certain to live with regrets. In the cult classic *City Slickers,* Billy Crystal's character realizes that life flies by. His sixth-grade son invites him to speak at dad's day in his class, so he blurts this out:

> Value this time in your life, kids, because … [life] goes by so quickly.
>
> When you're a teenager you think you can do anything, and you do.
>
> Your twenties are a blur.
>
> Your thirties, you raise a family, you make a little money, and you think to yourself, *What happened to my twenties?*
>
> Your forties, you grow a little potbelly, you grow another chin. The music starts to get too loud, and one of your old girlfriends from high school becomes a grandmother.
>
> Your fifties, you have minor surgery. You'll call it a procedure, but it's a surgery.
>
> Your sixties, you have major surgery. The music is still loud, but it doesn't matter because you can't hear it anyway.

Seventies, you and the wife retire to Fort Lauderdale. You start eating dinner at two, lunch around ten, breakfast the night before. You spend most of your time wandering around the malls looking for the ultimate in soft yogurt and muttering, "How come the kids don't call?"

By your eighties, you've had a major stroke, and you end up babbling to some Jamaican nurse who your wife can't stand but who you call Mama.

Any questions?[8]

DOWNSIZE YOUR THINGS

Yeah, your things, not your thighs.

A friend of mine once described himself as a recovering materialist. Then he went on to say, "But the good thing about being a recovering materialist is that I still have a lot of really nice things." We have a hard time letting go of our cheap junk, don't we?

After I talked about "stuff" this past Sunday, a young woman said to me, "Palmer, I love what you had to say this morning. And I want you to know I'm already trying to live that way. Yesterday I had a garage sale and sold all my purses."

"Wow. How many was that?" I asked.

"Fifty."

"Fifty purses. How in the world did you have fifty purses?" I laughed. She was the Imelda Marcos of purses. "Well, I'm proud of you for selling all fifty of your purses."

"Actually I sold forty. I still need ten."

Funny. But it's a great start.

I keep challenging the people at The Grove to live simply. Live with less, I tell them. Live generously. Life works better that way. And they're starting to live that way.

When Sebastian walked into my office with a great big Jim Carrey smile and a giant ziplock bag of change and announced that it was his birthday, I thought we might become a generous church.

Sebastian said, "Pastor Palmer, today I'm eight years old, and I'm bringing you one hundred and eight dollars for mosquito nets for kids in Africa." His dad explained that Sebastian had been collecting change for months and wanted to make the delivery on his birthday. It was a great moment. As Sebastian handed me the bulging bag of change, he said with resolve, "Next year, on my ninth birthday, I'm bringing you one hundred and nine dollars." I love it.

At The Grove we talk about living generously, living simply … so that others can simply live. I've always hoped this way of life would become our culture, part of our DNA.

In September we challenged our people to leave their shoes at church and go home barefoot, so that their shoes could be given away to people in Liberia who had no shoes. We dubbed it Barefoot Sunday. My sons told me this was a bad idea; they said people would not come to church that Sunday.

On Barefoot Sunday my sons were wrong—The Grove was packed. On Barefoot Sunday more than two thousand pairs of shoes were left at the church. On Barefoot Sunday I thought, *Maybe we're becoming a generous church.*

Three weeks before Thanksgiving, we put 180 empty boxes in the lobby and asked people to take a box home, go shopping, and fill it for a family's Thanksgiving dinner … and include a turkey. All the boxes were gone before people arrived for the third service. The third-service people grumbled that they had no boxes to fill.

We put a hundred more boxes out the next Sunday. Those all disappeared as well. The Sunday before Thanksgiving, as I stood and watched a refrigerated semi fill with 280 boxes of Thanksgiving dinners for families in need, I thought, *We could be on our way to becoming a generous church.*

A month before Christmas, we told the people of The Grove that this Christmas we would take our church's first-ever Christmas Missions Offering. The project we chose was to rebuild the gymnasium at African Bible College in Yekepa, Liberia, which was destroyed during the civil war. We needed $50,000—in one offering—on one Sunday! The amount was staggering. Frightening. Audacious. It would take a miracle, I told the people of The Grove.

On December 20 our people gave to help rebuild buildings and lives in Liberia, but instead of giving $50,000, they gave $110,000, and I thought, *We just might be a generous church.*

This Sunday, today, a couple stopped me after the second service, slipped a hundred-dollar bill in my hand, and said, "Please give this to someone who needs it." I said, "I will. I have no idea who, but I promise I will do that." After the third service a young man stopped to say hi. I knew that his wife had just lost her job and life was tight, and it hit me—*today they need this hundred dollars more than anyone else I know.* So I slipped the bill into his pocket and said, "A generous person at The Grove wants me to give this to you."

Today I realized we are a generous church.

Generosity really is a part of The Grove culture.

I try to live that way.

I hope you will too.

If you have any aspirations of becoming that spiritually deep person, you will become less busy, own fewer things, and make more time for God.

It's that simple.

LETTER TO MY FATHER

Dear Daddy, my eyes keep leaking.
Your presence is what I'm seeking.
I keep trying to send a call.
The problem is my voice is on a fall.
I need you here.
Although, seeing you is my fear.
But, why did you leave me?

You were the person I always wanted to see.

Now all I have is broken dreams.

That is what it seems.

This year I'm turning sixteen.

But, I want it to be unseen.

I see no reason to celebrate.

For my reason is out of sight.[9]

Harley Brunswick

Chapter 8

THE HAND IN FRONT OF YOUR FACE

Jesus took her by the hand.
Luke 8:54[1]

I'm sick.

I've just finished reading a *New York Times* article on the tragic murders of an albino mother and her five-year-old son in Burundi. Both were killed by witch doctors for their body parts.[2]

This is possibly the most senseless crime I have ever heard of.

About ten years ago, belief spread in east Africa that eating the body parts of an albino will bring fortune and success. So witch doctors and medicine men began hunting albinos. Since 2007, seventy-one albinos have been killed in Tanzania alone. Tens of thousands have gone into hiding.[3] The entire notion is completely absurd—BUT IT'S NOT BEING STOPPED.

Here in the United States, we are rightfully angered when people are discriminated against because of the color of their skin. But if mothers and five-year-old boys are dying in Burundi because of their skin color, shouldn't we all be outraged?

The killers must be brought to justice so that a message is sent loud and clear: No person anywhere should die because of skin color.

One small step I am taking is to write to the president of Burundi to offer to help, in whatever way needed, to stop this atrocity.

AN OPEN LETTER TO THE PRESIDENT OF BURUNDI, PIERRE NKURUNZIZA

Dear President Nkurunziza,

I write to you with a heart saddened by the tragic murder of a Burundian mother and her five-year-old son.

I write to say that these killers must be brought to justice. And I write to encourage you to pour every possible resource into protecting the lives of the marginalized albinos in Burundi.

I know that you are a man of God. I know your heart is good. So I simply write to implore you to seek justice for the albinos of Burundi.

I write on behalf of Christians everywhere—please stop this senseless crime. I do not write to place blame or to judge; I write to encourage action.

I also write to offer the resources of every Christian in my country who cares about justice. I write to offer means to help educate a population that killing albinos is the worst kind of crime, the most senseless of crimes. Albinos, like all of us, are created by God, in His image, and they are loved and prized by God—it's just that their skin is a different color. And only sheer ignorance would cause anyone to believe that there is magic in their bones.

I offer the resources of every Christian in America who cares about justice to help shelter and protect the albinos of Burundi.

I write to offer to partner with you to rescue those whose lives are threatened because of the color of their skin.

May God's great hand of blessing be on your life as you continue to lead with wisdom.

Respectfully,
Dr. Palmer Chinchen

Like a smoggy day in Los Angeles, injustice is the dark cloud that turns God's beautiful creation gray. But here's the question that I hope haunts your soul: *Do you care?*

You see, it's very possible to skate through this life and never be bothered by the trouble in this world. Don't live that way.

Here's the truth: Because this culture tells us to care most about *me*, we end up caring very little about albino mothers in Burundi. I want to challenge you to live differently.

When you live most about *me,* you end up not being able to see past the hand at the end of your outstretched arm. It's like living in a gray fog so thick that you can only see *you.*

Don't live that way. The life most about *me* turns hollow. It's a shallow existence.

God will have a hard time using your life until you clear your world of the fog of self-centered living.

The problem, however, is that we are constantly told to make this life most about *you, me, I.* The people at Apple know this. That's why they put your name in front of all their new products—iPhone, iPad, iTouch, iMac … you get my point.

But the life after Christ, the beautiful life, is more about others than it is about me.

If you want clarity for your future, if you want to live the life you've always dreamed of living, then stop making your world so much about you. I'm sorry to be so blunt. But that's the way it is.

SEE THE OPPRESSION: THE TORAH

When you clear your world of the fog of *you,* your eyes will open to the needs of the oppressed.

The Bible recounts Moses' story of God liberating His people. The books of Moses (the first five books of the Bible) tell the story of God's people moving from slavery to freedom. My childhood home is Liberia, a country named for the liberty granted to slaves from America. Exodus is that same story for the Jews. Moses writes about God's complaint: "I have … seen the misery of my people.… I have heard them crying out.… I have come down to rescue them."[4] So he speaks the famous words to Pharaoh in Egypt: "Let my people go!"[5]

God is always for liberation …

- from addiction.
- from oppression.
- from disease.
- from poverty.
- from racism.
- from debt.
- from sin.

When liberation comes, something transformational happens. We move from being slaves to being children, from being homeless to having a homeland.

DEMAND JUSTICE: THE WISDOM BOOKS

In the first chapter of the book of Ecclesiastes, Solomon admits to his pursuit of the *me-centered* life. He writes:

> I thought in my heart, "Come now, I will test you with pleasure to find out what is good." …I tried cheering myself with wine, and embracing folly…. I undertook great projects: I built houses for myself and planted vineyards. I made gardens and parks and planted all kinds of fruit trees in them. I made reservoirs to water groves of flourishing trees…. I amassed silver and gold for myself, and the treasure of kings and provinces. I acquired men and women singers, and a harem

as well…. I denied myself nothing my eyes
desired; I refused my heart no pleasure…. Yet
when I surveyed all that my hands had done
and what I had toiled to achieve, everything was
meaningless, a chasing after the wind; nothing
was gained under the sun.[6]

Solomon had indulged in everything and anything he desired. He wore himself out on pleasure and leisure. Life was a wanton vacation … and he found it empty.

When life is all about *me,* it turns pretty hollow.

Then Solomon looks up. He looks beyond the fog of his selfish life, and this is what he sees: "I looked and saw all the oppression that was taking place under the sun: I saw the tears of the oppressed—and they have no comforter."[7]

In Proverbs, King Solomon writes about the heart of God: "Rescue the perishing; don't hesitate to step in and help. If you say, 'Hey, that's none of my business,' will that get you off the hook? Someone is watching you closely, you know—Someone not impressed with weak excuses."[8] He even tells God, "Make me the king of justice!"[9]

Injustice is the lack of justice and equity, the violation of the rights of another or others: unequal, wrong, unfair. Solomon complained about it four thousand years ago; it's absurdly frustrating that we still live in a world filled with injustice.

Just weeks ago, for example, a summer camp in Philadelphia was granted permission to take their kids swimming at a country club's pool as part of their summer program. But after one day in the pool, the camp was asked to not come back. You see the kids were black; the country club members were white.[10]

What's wrong with us that we try to live that way?

If this is God's concern, it must be ours. Jesus came to rescue us from the idea that somebody else will turn the tide.

You see, before Saul and David and Solomon, Israel was ruled by judges. But the judges were not always just. So we read things like, "In those days Israel had no king; everyone did as he saw fit."[11]

When you can lift your head and clear your world of the fog of self-centered living, you will see the world that matters to God. You will see, for example, the albino mothers in Burundi.

Don't ever forget this: God hates injustice, and He wants it stopped.

I think injustice keeps God up at night.

But seeking justice on behalf of the oppressed and victimized is doable. And *you* are part of God's plan for ending injustice in the world.

The entire Bible speaks of God's desire for justice.

SPEAK OUT: THE PROPHETS

As you continue through the Bible, the prophetic books tell the story of God's voice for the oppressed.

The prophets were shouters. In fact they operated much like an African town crier. They walked the streets and yelled out God's demand for justice. Jonah did that in Nineveh, and people listened.

The ancient prophet Isaiah shouted this in the streets: "Stop doing wrong, learn to do right! Seek justice, encourage the oppressed. Defend the cause of the fatherless, plead the case of the widow."[12]

And you know the famous words of the prophet Micah: "Act justly and … love mercy."[13]

In the same way, you are to be a voice for those silenced in their oppression. I just returned from two weeks of travel through Africa with my friend Scott, who paints images of Africans. He says his paintings are meant to be a voice for all who are silenced in Africa—a voice for all who have AIDS, all who live in shantytowns, all who drink filthy water, all who go barefoot, all who have been raped, all who are orphaned.

That's a lot of people to speak up for. Scott can't do it alone. God put you here to be a voice for everyone who is silent in affliction.

One of my local heroes is CNN reporter and Channel 3 anchor Mike Watkiss. Mike has made it his job to expose the sick men, in places like Colorado City, who force twelve-year-old girls to marry them.

It's rape.

Mike doesn't take crap from anyone. He's fearless in speaking out against this vile practice. I wish more Christian pastors and leaders were equally bold.

But here's the thing: We love to talk about our own problems … and rarely do we look up long enough to speak out about the problems of others.

Behaviorists call it narcissism. We all have a little bit of it in us. Do you know how long we typically listen to someone who's talking to us? Seven seconds. That's it. Seven seconds! For example, you run into a friend and say, "Hey, how've you been?" They answer, "Great. I just got back from Bali." Then they begin to tell you about Bali. But at seven seconds you stop listening and start thinking about your own connection to Bali. As soon as they pause to take a breath, you chime in, "I have an aunt who went to Bali. She bought me the most comfortable pair of hand-woven sandals I've ever owned...." At the seven-second mark, your friend will start thinking about sandals—*Sandals ... hey, I know a girl who glues bling on sandals....*

It's called *verbal salad*. It's the tendency in all of us to make conversations—life—mostly about me.

And when it comes to problems, we just love to talk about our problems. Ask anyone over thirty how they're doing, and you get a medical history not even their mother cares about. They'll try to tell you why they need Flomax and Metamucil and prunes and a whole lot more that you couldn't care less about.

The person that God uses talks more about others than themselves. They praise and promote others with their words. They can listen—really listen. They talk about the problems of this world more than the petty gripes of life.

SHOW COMPASSION: THE GOSPELS

As we turn the pages of the Bible from the Old to the New Testament, we come to the Gospels. The Gospels are God's story of compassion.

At the very center of the justice story are the birth, life, ministry, death, and resurrection of Jesus Christ. He said it Himself: "The Spirit of the Lord is on me, because he has anointed me to preach good news to the poor ... [and] proclaim freedom for the prisoners and recovery of sight for the blind [and] to release the oppressed."[14]

Loving God and loving your neighbor are inseparable. Someone asked Jesus, "Who is my neighbor?" So he told them about a man beaten down and left on the roadside. That's your neighbor.[15]

Jesus knew we all tend to walk around the needy, more concerned about our own life problems and needs. Compassion requires
seeing the world through the eyes of another. We are not naturally
wired that way.

Educators have begun using babies to teach grade-school kids
about compassion. In Victoria, British Columbia, for example,
twenty babies will go classroom to classroom, wearing T-shirts labeled
Teacher, to teach kids about empathy. Kids observe the baby then
talk about why "their" baby seems cranky or happy or inquisitive
or afraid. The Roots of Empathy program is designed to help kids
become more observant of what others are feeling and, as a result, act
more kindly—"The program helps to create a culture of caring and
compassion among children through the eyes of a baby."[16]

THE CLOUD OF NARCISSISM

You see, even children have to learn to see the needs of others, because
we are all born with this natural tendency to see only our own desires
and needs, and live blind to the needs of those around us.

Living this way is imperative, not only for the sake of Christ but
for your sake. Narcissistic living will suck your soul dry. That's the
lesson of the Greek myth of Narcissus and his infatuation with his
own appearance. It eventually sickened him to death.

And that's what happens spiritually and even socially when we
make this life mostly about *me*.

I just spent two weeks in Liberia with Shane. He's six foot eight
and was a beast in the middle on our basketball team. Shane's a car
dealer and does pretty well. Before we left Liberia, Shane told me,
"When I first landed in Liberia, all I saw when I looked at people was

what they had and didn't have—the bare feet, tattered clothes, and mud huts. But now after two weeks of getting to know Liberians, I'm really seeing them. Now when I talk to them, I see their faces, their smiles, their joy. That's what has really struck me about this trip, I've stopped seeing what people have, and I'm seeing who people are."

One of the most troubling images for me from Haiti, just days after the devastating earthquake, was that of a cruise ship listlessly floating in a bay with dozens of vacationers splashing in the water all around. I couldn't make sense of it. How in the world can you play in the water when just around the jetty, people are trapped under piles of concrete, suffocating to death? How do you get in line at the all-you-can-eat, midnight buffet when outside the cabin window, families have not eaten for days?

The entire notion was absolutely absurd.

Jesus always responded with compassion to the needs of hurting people: the sick, the blind, the lame, the poor, the afflicted, the diseased, the perishing. Henri Nouwen names Jesus "The Wounded Healer," because by His wounds and in His woundedness, He heals you and me and everyone else who hurts.

Jesus brought dignity to the marginalized, He gave respect to the poor, He noticed the afflicted, He paid attention to the outcast.

Here's the *good news* of the Gospels—you can make a difference.

Begin caring more about people in this world who hurt.

Begin to live full of the compassion of Christ.

SHARE HOPE: THE LETTERS

The final pages of the Bible are filled with letters—letters that tell God's story of hope.

> They will be his people, and God himself will be
> with them and be their God. He will wipe every
> tear from their eyes. There will be no more death
> or mourning or crying or pain.[17]

The letters are about the church. And Christ meant for the church to be the hope of the world. It really is. His message of life and hope is meant to be blasted out from the church.

I'll say it again: *The church is the hope of the world.*

If you are a pastor or a Christian leader, your role is so big. Don't ever think your calling is small. If you are Christ follower, your role is so big. You are part of a movement, a force that God wants to use to turn this world upside down.

That's why I say the church—that's you, Christians everywhere—is the hope of the world.

BEAT

Mind is churning,
soul is shaken.

Heart is burning,
bodies overtaken.
Lost for words...
Hungry for assistance...
Vision is blurred...
I see pain from a distance...
Beat by words...
Floating in my head...
Thoughts are absurd...
Becoming thoughts overfed...
Break from this silence...
Break from these chains...
Prevent me from violence...
Prevent me from pain...
God give me Ambition...
God give me Hope...
To face this opposition...
That I may learn to cope...
Joy slowly fades...
Sorrow slowly creeps...
Scarred by the blades...
Slowly cutting as I sleep...
Beaten by these tears...
Beaten by these cries...
Overcome by my fears...
Misled by these lies...........[18]

Brian Misinale

SELAH

Chapter 9

YOU

I love—you!
Psalm 18:1[1]

You—yes, *you*—are a piece of heaven on earth.

Liberia was in chaos. Not long after my wife and I evacuated our home in northern Liberia, where Charles Taylor and his rebel army first invaded the country, his soldiers advanced on the capital city of Monrovia and put it under siege.

Along with hundreds of thousands of other Liberians, my good friend Mawolo was trapped in the city, the middle of a war zone.

Monrovia was still controlled by the ruling president, Samuel Doe. In trying to squelch the uprising, Doe went on a genocidal rampage in the city. He and his Krahn (Doe's tribe) soldiers began slaughtering everyone they could find from the tribes that had allied with Charles Taylor, particularly the Mono and Geo people. In his bloodiest moment, Doe, along with several dozen commandos, crashed through the doors of a large Lutheran church where hundreds of Mono and Geo people had fled for sanctuary. Trapped in the siege, they believed they would be safe in a church.

But Doe had long since turned his back on God. He had named himself the *Zoe*, chief of all Grand Devils and witch doctors. Doe thought he was god.

In the dark this witch doctor and his men raided the church with M16s and machetes. While Doe and his generals hacked people inside the church to death, those who tried to escape were shot down by soldiers waiting outside. More than five hundred men, women, and children were executed that night.

The mood in the city was savage. Mawolo knew he needed to escape. So risking his life, he slipped through rebel lines and began the long walk through the jungle to the safety of neighboring Sierra Leone.

However, on his third day of walking, as he neared the Sierra Leone border, he stumbled upon a rebel checkpoint. Before he could run, the boy soldiers had their guns on him. "Get on the ground, soldier-man," the boys screamed, accusing him of being one of Doe's Krahn soldiers. Their pupils were open wide from drugs, and their fingers twitched on the triggers of their M16s as the boys circled around Mawolo laying on the ground.

Taylor's boy soldiers were notoriously vicious. They killed indis-
criminately. Their commanders fed them heroin and cocaine so their
battles were fought in a mental fog. They seemed to have utterly lost
their conscience. The boys believed the medicine man's lies that his juju
would make the bullets miss them. He told them if they fought naked
they would be invisible—one entire battalion was appropriately named
the butt-naked battalion. Others wore women's wigs and nightgowns
that flowed when they ran; they said it made them look like the spirits.

"What you talking about?" Mawolo protested. "I'm Loma, and I'm
not a soldier-man. I'm a student at African Bible College in Yekepa!"

"If you're Loma, speak Loma or you will die right here," one of
the boys with guns retorted.

He spoke some Loma, but this still didn't help much because
none of the boys could understand a word of Loma.

"That thing you speaking sounds like nonsense," one blurted out.
"You look like a soldier man running away to Sierra Leone. Let's kill
him!"

Mawolo says he knew things were really bad then. From the
ground he could see the skulls of their victims mounted on poles on
each side of the bamboo gate. His mind raced with panic as he tried
to think of a way out … when suddenly he heard the sweetest sound
of his life: "Mawolo!" Someone knew his name, and right then, fac-
ing death, it meant everything.

Out of the corner of his eye, Mawolo caught a glimpse of a rebel
commander walking up the road.

"My man, get up!" Mawolo looked up again to see Big Momo.
He knew Big Momo well. They had banged around under the boards
almost every afternoon in the ABC gym in Yekepa.

As he stood Big Momo gave him a giant bear hug. It felt really good.

"What's going on here?" Momo asked.

"These pekins want to kill me!" Mawolo answered as he stood.

Big Momo turned and let the boy soldiers have it: "What's wrong with you foolish boys? I should beat you guys with a switch. This is my good friend Mawolo. He's one of Liberia's best basketball players."

Mawolo had never been so happy to see a basketball player from a rival school.

When someone knows our name we feel known, special, wanted, loved, even rescued.

GOD LOVES *YOU*

A pastor in the Northwest has been getting publicity out of saying, "God hates you." He really believes it and uses some odd concoction of Old Testament passages to support his bizarre theology.

Can I tell you the truth? God's love for you is as deep as the ocean and more than you'll ever know.

And God does not love you passively, but personally. He does not simply know the flock or the crowd—He knows each sheep, each person. He knows you, and He knows you by name. That is what Jesus Himself tells us: "The sheep listen to his voice. He calls his own sheep by name and leads them out. When he has brought out all his own, he goes on ahead of them, and his sheep follow him because they know his voice.... I know my sheep and my sheep know me."[2]

When I look at a flock of sheep, I see ... a flock of sheep. When a shepherd looks at the flock, he sees individual needs and unique qualities. When I glance at a stadium crowd, I see ... a crowd. Not

God. He looks upon the billions on earth, and He sees you and me. He sees the beauty in each one of us. Each person is special, important, with their own significant story that God knows by heart. He loves each one of us by name.

The Christ always called His people by name:

- Walking down the beach recruiting his posse He shouted to two brothers, "James, John, drop your nets, it's time to catch people."[3]
- When He saw the corrupt accountant in the tree, He said, "Zacchaeus get down here with me right now, let's head to your house for lunch, I'm hungry!"[4]
- As tears ran down His cheeks because His friend was dead and buried in a dark cave, He yelled to him, "Lazarus, get up and get out!"[5]
- When His friends were looking for His dead body in the garden, He said, "Mary, I'm right here!"[6]
- After His biggest fan had abandoned Him, He sat next to a charcoal fire with him and asked, "Peter, do you really love me?"[7]

He calls you by name like that, because your name means the world to God.

BLACK TISSUE BOXES

God loves you like this:

Harriet Lerner was ten and her sister Susan was twelve. It was Christmas, and Harriet wanted a bicycle, and her sister wanted a set of encyclopedias. But it had been a tough year, so when she came downstairs that Christmas morning, there was just one present under the tree for each of the girls.

She and her sister opened their single present as their parents sat watching on the couch. Their gifts were identical—ugly black metal tissue boxes with tacky hand-painted roses scattered on the surface. Tears immediately welled up in Harriet's eyes; the present was awful.

Just as tears began to roll down her cheeks, Susan exclaimed, "What a great present—I've heard about these tissue boxes; they're painted by trained monkeys!" Suddenly Harriet saw the boxes in a new light. She found herself liking the boxes. And for years she would tell friends about the boxes painted by trained monkeys.

Harriet believed this story into college. But one break she returned home and was cleaning out Susan's closet when she came upon an English composition her sister had written in high school, titled *The Tissue Box*. She sat down and read the short story. Her sister recounted the Christmas just as Harriet remembered, except for when she got to the part about the trained monkeys.

Her sister wrote that, when they opened their presents and saw the ugly painted tissue boxes, she remembered that her father had a friend who painted boxes as a hobby. She knew her parents hated charity, but that was all they had.

When she noticed her sister's tears and knew the tears would hurt her parents as well, she concocted the story about trained monkeys.

After seeing her sister Harriet smile again, she rushed upstairs and cried in her pillow.

Susan, Harriet realized, took the pain for both of them. She carried the weight so Harriet could be free to treasure her black box.[8]

God loves you like that. He's sent His Son to carry your pain and your burdens.

Your life is no accident. You are not here by happenstance. God put you here on purpose. He makes no mistakes. Your life has profound meaning. God sees in you what no one else has ever seen: "You are the only you he made.... You are it! And if you aren't you, we don't get you. The world misses out. You are heaven's Halley's Comet; we have one shot at seeing you shine."[9]

There is nothing ordinary about you. The psalmist writes, "He fashions [your heart] individually."[10] Jesus says it like this, "What's the price of a pet canary? Some loose change, right? And God cares what happens to it even more than you do. He pays even greater attention to you, down to the last detail—even numbering the hairs on your head! So don't be intimidated by all this bully talk. You're worth more than a million canaries."[11]

YOU ARE A CHILD OF GOD

Here is the most central truth about your identity: You are a child of God. A child of the King of Kings. Before your own mother or father knew you, God knew your name.

That we are called children of God is made clear throughout the Bible. Israel's most treasured identity is that they were children of God. Jesus used the word *Abba,* which is Aramaic for "father," or more literally, "daddy," a rather informal name for the God of the universe. Most first-century Jews would consider this familiarity irreverent and unacceptable. Devout Jews rarely even used God's Hebrew name Yahweh. But Abba was Jesus' relationship with His heavenly Father.[12] Jesus knew what it felt like to be named a child of God. God spoke out loud and said, "This is my Son, whom I love."[13]

Several great truths are buried in this doctrine. First, one can never choose to be a child. Childhood happens to us. God has chosen us. What a beautiful hope and peace this truth brings. Second, one can never cease to be a son or daughter. Today, driving home from his high school golf match, my seventeen-year-old son had his first car accident. He was petrified that I was going to be angry with him—yell, shout, be mad. So when he called he said, "Dad, I just rear-ended another car … but I shot a thirty-eight today!" … hoping the thirty-eight in nine holes would make me forget about the thousand-dollar deductible.

But it's just a car. By all means, I love him more than any car I'll ever own. I don't think I felt one moment of anger. I was just glad he was okay … and as I drove to the accident, we spent the next five minutes on the phone talking about his golf round. The bottom line is this: Nothing my four sons ever do will cause me to love them less, let alone change their status as my sons. And it is exactly the same in our relationship with God. Nothing you or I will ever do will cause Him to stop loving us. Nothing. When you are His child, you are His forever:

> "He invites you to bask in his deep delight over you, even in the midst of your darkest defeat. He invites you to accept the safety and security of his embrace. He longs to listen to you, even when you don't have the words to talk. He is your Abba, and according to Jesus, you are his beloved child."[14]

Jesus tells two parables, one about a lost sheep and the other about a lost son. While the sheep and son are lost, the shepherd and the father have absolutely no peace. The shepherd drops everything to search tirelessly for his lamb. The father scans the horizon waiting for his son's return. When the lamb and son are found, something profound happens—a party is thrown. This is cause for great celebration. The treasured lamb is back. The loved son has returned. Break out the Martinelli!

A celebration just like this took place, or will take place, for you. The writer of Revelation says that, on the day your name was written in the Lamb's Book of Life, the angels in heaven celebrated. They celebrated because of you. They celebrated your name. They celebrated that you are a child of God. If you have never allowed God to be your Father, He waits, and a party is waiting to break out for you.

The Bible also tells us that God loves you like a *precious jewel*. In the Song of Songs you are described as *jewels around His neck*.[15]

One beautiful Hebrew word says it all: *segulah*. *Segulah* means "precious" or "treasured." Jewish people will name their baby girls *Segulah*, because they are like precious jewels.

Old Testament writers like Moses used this word to explain how you are prized by God: "You will be my *treasured* [segulah] possession."[16] The word image associated with *segulah* is that of a king who keeps his most treasured jewels beneath his throne; each day he pulls out the chest and runs his fingers through the gold and silver, admiring it, treasuring it. And *segulah* explains the exclusive possession entitled to the owner—it belongs to him and no one else. "Out of all the peoples on the face of the earth, the LORD has chosen you to be his *treasured* [segulah] possession."[17]

GOD LOVES YOUR NAME

All of us like to hear our own names spoken. We like them pro-
nounced correctly, and we don't enjoy people making fun of our
names. I've always gotten the business over the last name Chinchen,
so I will admit my sensitivity. Someone called our home not long
ago, and when I answered, he asked, "Is Homer Chicken in?"

"We're not friends, are we?" I answered. "We've never met, have
we? Because that wasn't even close!" I think he was selling time-shares
in Sedona.

Soon after I met my wife, Veronica, we ended up in the Biola
University cafeteria, having lunch. I had a pile of Chinese food in
front of me, and, wanting to be funny, she leaned over and asked,
"So, since your last name is Chinchen, do you like Chinese food?"

Without hesitating, I pointed at her hot dog and snidely asked,
"Since your last name is Bernard, do you like dog food?" She wasn't
nearly as amused as I was by my clever comeback!

The fact is, Veronica's name is rich with beautiful meaning—her
name means "truth and purity." And all you have to do is meet sweet
Veronica once, and you will know her life is like that—full of truth
and purity. Our names say a lot about us.

Palmer means "pilgrim." I kind of like that because that's what
the ancients called expatriates—and I like to think of myself as an
expatriate. A pilgrim was only just passing through, and I've never
really known where to call home. I feel restless in this life; I hope that's
a good thing. And maybe it is, because I don't think God ever meant
for us to get too comfortable in this life and mistake it for home.

My good friend Corey has taught me a valuable life lesson.
Whenever he sits down at a restaurant, the first thing he does is

ask the server his or her name. Then, for the next hour and a half or so, he uses that person's name like he's known the server for years. It's brilliant. The server smiles more. You get free stuff, and your whole dinner experience changes simply because you cared enough to know someone's name. Corey says Brennan Manning taught him this. The server's name matters to God, so it should matter to us.

God calls us and knows us by name. He knows our name well because we are important to Him and He has a wonderful future waiting for us. Isaiah the prophet explains this wonderful truth like this: "I have written your name on my hand."[18]

God doesn't just know your name; He loves your name. Your name matters to God. And maybe there's not a whole lot we are supposed to do with this truth except enjoy it. Relish it. Embrace it. Love the fact that God knows us intimately. Not casually or passively, but closely.

Last week I found these words mysteriously, beautifully inscribed in red lipstick on our bathroom mirror: *I ♥ Palmer.* That's me. Who would write such a thing? I was pretty sure it wasn't Scott, the carpet guy. I didn't think it was one of my high school sons, and since our next-door neighbor, Shane, who often walked into our house unannounced, had just moved … it had to be my wife!

When I saw the writing in red, my first thought was, *I am lucky. I am lucky because somebody loves me! And this beautiful somebody loves me by name.* For some reason, it seemed really nice to see my name next to the *I ♥*, rather than the generic *you.*

The words stayed on the mirror for a week. My two younger sons kept asking, "Why did Mom write on the mirror? Why is that there?

What does it mean?" They seemed very troubled by the mysterious handwriting on the wall—in red lipstick, no less. I told them, "That means your mom thinks your dad is hot. And don't ever forget that. That's what that means." They didn't seem convinced.

A week later I walked in, and Veronica was wiping the mirror clean. "I have to clean the bathroom," she said apologetically. "Oh, that's cool," I answered nonchalantly. I acted like it really didn't matter, but the truth was, I wanted the words to remain on the mirror forever. I wanted the reminder that somebody loves me—somebody loves *Palmer*.

We all need that, don't we? And we have that love. God loves us by name. Our name means the world to Him. It always has, and it always will.

Insert your name in this Bible passage:

> *How great is the love the Father has lavished*
> *on _____, that _____*
> *should be called [a child] of God! And that is what*
> *_____ [is]!*[19]

You

are

a

child

of

God … and that means the world.

NEVER AGAIN

The sun sets on my love,
The sun rises on my love,
My heart heats in the darkness,
My pulse quickens at the sound of your voice.

I remember the first touch,
It won't be like that again,
I remember your last kiss,
Never again, never again.

Frozen silence in your bed,
Screams of terror to wake the dead
Heard down the hall in the emergency room,
Day by day, night comes too soon.

Draw me a bath that is pure and clean
To wash these sins away from me.
Away from my heart, away from my skin,
Never again, never again.[20]

Chloe Sparacino

Chapter 10

MERCY DROPS

Love mercy.
Micah 6:8

Mercy drops.

Like the song we used to sing in Sunday school—"Mercy drops round us are falling...."

But what ever happened to mercy? No one talks about it much anymore, not even preachers and pastors, and it sure seems like this world is short on mercy.

If there was just a bit more mercy to go around, *I think* ...

... baseball umpires would, now and then, give batters a fourth strike.

… when defensive linemen come charging around the blind side, they would yell, "Hey, heads up!"

… banks would lower mortgage payments.

… motorcycle cops would smile and say, "Easy, lead foot; I might have to cite you next time. Haha!"

… orphaned babies in Haiti would be taken home.

… lonely people would have more friends.

… single mothers would feel wanted.

But for the most part, we choose not to live that way.

Gary Thomas, who writes widely on the subject of spiritual formation, wrote a book entitled *Sacred Pathways*. In it he reminds us we all pursue God in different ways—we are all wired different spiritually.[1] Some take the activist pathway, some the traditionalist path; some are contemplative, some intellectual—but the pathway less traveled is *mercy*.

Jesus talked much about mercy. He once ended up in a conversation with a lawyer who was asking about true religion. So Jesus challenged the lawyer with an illustration of a man beaten and left on the roadside. He said a rabbi walked by and a Levite walked by, but then a Samaritan stopped and bandaged the man's wounds, and picked him up, and took him to safety. Jesus then turned back to the lawyer and asked, "Who is my neighbor?" In other words, which person showed true religion? And the lawyer answered with these words: "The one who showed him *mercy*."[2]

You see, Jesus' point was this: If you really know God, if you really are committed to His kingdom, if you really mean what you say you believe, then you will live full of mercy.

IF I HAVE NO MERCY …

The world we live in only works if we live with mercy.

Because *if I have no mercy* …

> … my kids have to be perfect.
>
> … my husband or wife will never get it right.
>
> … my coworkers are always incompetent.
>
> … the rising sun will never bring a new day—and the writer of Lamentations reminds us that the mercies of God are new every morning.[3]
>
> … I will never forgive and always remain bitter.

Last month while I was in Liberia, I became reacquainted with Jarbah. Jarbah and I grew up together deep in the Sappo jungle, but I hadn't seen Jarbah in over thirty years. It was good to laugh over dinner as we swapped stories about our childhood in the bush. Then I asked about his mother. "She's dead," he told me. "The Tiagen tribe, our people's enemy, killed her during the civil war."

I had no idea the war had reached that deep into the Liberian interior, but the fighting in the cities had given tribes across the country new excuses to settle ancient scores.

I said, "Jarbah, I'm really sorry, I had no idea."

"It's okay, Palmer. I've forgiven them."

He had; he really had. God had a grip on Jarbah's heart. He's a powerful man in Liberia, but he has a deeply tender heart that's full of mercy.

"Palmer, my people, the Sappo tribe, want me to take revenge. They keep telling me, 'Jarbah, let's go find those people who killed your mother and our mothers. It's time to take revenge.' But my people are angry with me," he continued, "because I won't take revenge, and I keep telling them it's time to forgive."

If I have no mercy, I will live full of bitterness and never live full of peace.

The next morning we got up with the sun to drive the final seven hours into the bush to visit our childhood home.

Hundreds of people came out to welcome my family and Jarbah. A ceremony had been planned for the occasion; it had been more than thirty years since we had been back to our home in the jungle.

As my father was giving a welcome speech, he began to quote Scripture. And just as he began to speak words from the Bible, I heard the drums begin to beat. The Grand Devil was coming. It was juju versus Jesus.

In many ways, the Grand Devil represents the evil that happens in the jungle. In the jungle it has always been the juju of the witch doctors and Grand Devils versus the truth and power of Jesus Christ. But during the horrible years of civil war, juju spread wildly. The Grand Devils promised rebel fighters and boy soldiers magical protection from bullets if they would participate in their ceremonies and make a sacrifice—sometimes human. Liberia has always been a Christian nation, but juju became the faith of war.

It was the Grand Devil and his followers who wanted Jarbah to take revenge on the Tiagen.

And now that Jesus' message of mercy and forgiveness was again being carried back into the jungle, the Grand Devil was vexed. His power was threatened because Jesus was back.

The Grand Devil came dancing, but the county superintendent shut him down. He stopped the noisy protest. He, too, spoke words from the Bible. Jesus was back. The people were ready to live differently.

MERCY IS NEAR TO THE HEART OF GOD

Writers throughout the Bible talk about God's mercy. In the Old Testament, David writes, "The Lord is full of pity and mercy."[4] And then for twenty-six lines in a row, David says, "His mercy endures forever."[5] Then He is described as "gracious, and full of compassion; slow to anger, and of great mercy."[6] The writers of the New Testament continue this theme. Paul, for example, says that "God … is rich in mercy."[7]

Around the world people still know the great mercy of God. In Kenya they say, "If the cow has no tail, God will keep the flies away."

Here's why mercy is such a critical commodity. All Christians sin. Our sin is great. But God's mercy is greater than our sin. God's mercy is enormous, limitless, and offered to everyone.

What is most amazing about God is how full of mercy He is; He is so, so full of mercy. There's no limit to God's mercy. His mercy is somewhere in the category of infinity because no end to His mercy is ever reached; His mercy is never exhausted, never used up.

The ancient Hebrew prophet Micah famously asks the rhetorical question, "What can we bring to the LORD? What kind of offerings should we give him? Should we bow before God with offerings of yearling calves? Should we offer him thousands of rams and ten thousand rivers of olive oil?"[8]

But Micah knows this is not what God wants…. God doesn't want your things; He wants your life:

"And what does the LORD require of you? To act justly and to love *mercy* and to walk humbly with your God."[9]

THE MERCY GENERATION

This generation gets it. Fritz Kling observes, "Younger Christians are often ambivalent about the institutional church, but completely committed to Mercy."[10]

I tried to tell Marco that the construction team leaving for Haiti was for men. He looked offended. Marco's seventeen. I told him he would be sleeping outside and in a tent. He said, "So?" I could tell that nothing I told him was dissuading him from wanting to join the team leaving for Haiti … so I found his mother. "I don't think it's totally safe in Haiti; I don't think it's a good idea for Marco to go to Haiti." She looked at me and smiled. "Marco doesn't care. He says he has to go."

Marco went. Next month he leaves for Malawi to hang mosquito nets in huts where children have no nets.

I think we all need to stop trying to tell this generation how to live their faith, because they get it. They are very passionate about living out the mercy of God. They are mobile. They don't wait for institutions and organizations; they make things happen at the grassroots level. They grow coffee, they start microbusinesses, they teach, they'll go anywhere, they care for orphans, they feed hungry kids—they do the work of the cross.

TODAY IS NOT TOO SOON

As our 737 skimmed over the brilliant green water of the Caribbean, headed for Santo Domingo, I read these words in a USA today article:

"A number of colleges have shown interest in helping Haiti after its earthquake. But they're being discouraged," because it's too soon.[11]

I was on my way to Haiti. But our 737, packed with spring-break college students leaving the United States to serve, will only go as far as the Dominican Republic. The dozens of students on our flight will never make it to Haiti because they, like so many others, are being fed lines like, "It's too soon for service trips to Haiti."

If today is too soon, then when will the day be right? What greater disaster must a nation suffer before the time is right? The article states that the CIDI (an ominous-sounding acronym for the Center for International Disaster Information) is advising volunteers to "wait until conditions are better to serve … at least one year."

What tragic irony. How will conditions ever get any better unless people go and help make them better?

The article implies that volunteers and college students will use "valuable resources" in Haiti that can be better used by someone else. That statement would be funny if it wasn't so sad. I'll bet cash money the person who made this statement at the CIDI has never set foot in Haiti. Believe me, I've been there. Even in Port-au-Prince there's enough bread and bananas and goat (yep, our last team had goat in Port-au-Prince) to feed college students.

This same kind of reasoning is what vexed me when buildings came crashing down in January. It took five days of sitting and watching and assessing and evaluating before our government felt it was "safe" enough to allow earthquake rescue workers into Port-au-Prince to begin digging through the rubble for survivors. FIVE DAYS! I was sick. We should have had people there in five hours. Literally.

Sean Penn is a stud. He was in Haiti, yelling for America to get down there and get people out of the mud and rain. He built a camp for forty-five thousand Haitians who have lost their homes. I caught him on CNN. He said, "Get down here, or people will die!" He's right.[12]

I hope you see what I'm saying: Wherever or whatever the need, circumstances will never be perfect or perfectly safe. But go anyway. That's when you're needed most.

Now is the time for mercy.

GOD WHISPERS, *SHOW MORE MERCY*

Justice is necessary and good, but justice is only legitimate if you first live full of mercy. It's one thing to live as a person who demands justice, but it's quite another to live as a person full of mercy.

People who know a merciful God will love mercy. And so I ask, "Are you really one of those who truly loves mercy?"

If you live without mercy, you will live alone.

Sometimes it's the withholding of mercy that hurts the most. We do that to punish others, to get even, to settle a score.

Jesus gave an example like that: He says a man is in great debt to the king, so he begs for mercy. The king's heart is soft, so he pardons the debt. As the man is on his way home, he comes across a poor man who owes him money—not much, just enough to make him mad. The poor man pleads for mercy, but the man who was just given mercy shows none.[13]

When you read the Old Testament, you can't help but notice that King David's heart was tender and full of mercy. When he was young, for example, he had the opportunity to kill his enemy Saul. Saul was actually in the middle of a hunt to kill David when he took a restroom break in a cave, the very cave David was hiding in. As Saul rested on a rock in the dark cave, David's men kept whispering, "Kill him, kill him, kill him now!" But David heard God's whisper: "Show mercy, show mercy now." So he took out his knife and cut a corner from Saul's robe and let him live.[14]

When David writes the famous Psalm 23, he writes about mercy: "Mercy shall follow me all the days of my life."[15]

Maybe we should all pray for more mercy. I know that's what God wants. That's what He's whispering to you.

> When he leaves his Razor scooter behind your car … and you back over it, God is whispering, *Show him mercy.*
>
> When she comes home with a D, God is whispering, *Show her mercy.*
>
> When he loses his job because he's difficult, God is whispering, *Show him mercy.*
>
> When she makes a snide remark about you, God is whispering, *Show her mercy.*
>
> When she breaks her promise, God is whispering, *Show her mercy.*
>
> This world needs more mercy.

Like Elijah in the desert, we all end up desperate and need drops of mercy. Ask God for people who show you mercy, like …

… the friend who shares his frequent flyer miles.

… the neighbor who brings you a meal when your children are sick.

… the banker who lowers your monthly mortgage payment (I need her number).

… the teacher who lets you retake a test.

… the boss who gives you another chance.

… the friend who forgives your harsh words.

… the husband who remembers to say "I love you."

FROM HEAVEN TO EARTH

In a previous book, *True Religion*, I wrote about taking pieces of heaven to places of hell on earth. People often ask, "What are pieces of heaven; what do you mean by that?" Here's what I mean: In this world, in this life, God gives us glimpses of heaven. Life as God intended is not a far-off place and time. The kingdom of heaven, Jesus said, is here! It's all around you. It's in you. The kingdom of heaven is meant to be lived out by God's people—right now.

So when we live a certain way, we bring the kingdom of God to earth; we live out heaven right now. (Yes, heaven is real and eternal, but kingdom living starts here.) This happens when we show mercy, for example, or experience the mercy of God. The case is the same with *love, attention, empathy, compassion, goodness.* Over the next several chapters we will examine each of these mercy drops from heaven.

The following chapters are not just about living *in* the mercy of God; they are most about living *out* the mercy of God.

You are His means of mercy.

GOD, PLEASE HELP ME

She stares blindly into the night
fighting the tears she knows
will not come
She holds her own hand
because she has no one else's
hand to hold
And whispers to herself
to make it to the morning

The scars on her wrists tell
what she cannot say
And we can all see
that she's wasting away
The razor kisses her lovelessly
and Ana refuses to leave her
even for a moment

'God, please help me!'
she screams
so silently
'I am weak,
I am lost,

I need a Saviour.
And only you,
God,
only you can save me ...'
she takes a breath
'Save me from myself'[16]

Scott Erickson

PART III

BRIGHT MORNINGS

His mercies ... are new every morning.
Lamentations 3:22–23[1]

Back to the dark night on the Kenya–Tanzania border:

Like I was saying, approaching quickly from my right is a tall dark man with a spear in one hand and a machete in the other. My heart is racing, there's no wind in my pipes to yell, I turn to run, when our Maasai laughs and says, "This is my uncle; he's the resort's night watchman." It wasn't funny. I was fine, but I think John was really scared.

The place is shut down for the night, but the Maasai's uncle rummages for a key, lets us into a small but crisply clean bungalow, and says, "That will be twenty-five dollars for the night."

I balk. "Twenty-five dollars? That's too much. We've missed half the night already. How about twenty?"

John looks at me like I am insane. "He's got a spear in his hand. Just pay the man," he says under his breath.

So I pay him, and our Maasai quietly slips back into the darkness.

I lay in bed in our small bungalow on the Kenya–Tanzania border and wait for daylight. I've never been so glad to see the sun rise as I was that next morning.

I had a restless night's sleep waiting for daylight. Perhaps I had forgotten the simple reality that nights don't last forever. They never do. The sun always rises. New days bring new beginnings with the light of the sun. Maybe that is why I like mornings best.

I walk outside that morning in Namanga to find I'm in one of the quaintest resorts I've visited in Africa. The Maasai was right; something beautiful was buried in the darkness.

NIGHTS ARE NOT FOREVER

Daylight is coming, dark nights never last forever, and valleys are not meant for dwelling. David says, "I walk *through* the valley of the shadow of death"[2]—God did not intend for him to remain there. He walked through it—with God.

Find comfort and strength from those who have wandered through darkness before you. Give strength to those who will follow.

Jesus said, "I am the light of the world. Whoever follows me will never walk in darkness, but will have the light of life."[3]

TWO WAYS TO LIVE

God wants to fill your life with meaning and purpose. You are not meant to simply exist; you are meant to thrive, to really live.

You see, there's a way to live in which you just get by—or there's a way to really live. You can get by in the gray days, or you can really live for Jesus Christ.

a. Just Exist

You can say you don't need God, you don't believe in God … and simply exist, put in your time. You can be the empty bubble on a sea of nothingness. But the human soul turns septic when God is absent. Life will turn into a monotonous drudge.

If your life has been painted gray, then let me tell you about Jesus Christ. If your life has been drab, let me tell you about a new way to *really* live.

Stop living the life you don't want to live.

How do you want to live every day for the rest of your life?

Start to live that way.

Stop living a life you can't stand. You don't have to.

If you are just existing, you're not living.

You can live the way you dream of living (and it has nothing to do with money), or you can live a nightmare.

b. Live Full of God

Live full of God, and you will live full of life. Life doesn't have to be lived in the grays; God waits to fill your life with beauty and meaning in the most unexpected ways and in the most unlikely places.

Do you know, for example, flowers are delivered daily to Newark Airport's Terminal B men's room?[4] Have you heard that flowers can count? The Venus flytrap, for example, has three hairs. If a fly steps on one, nothing happens. If a fly steps on two, its dirty life is snuffed out.[5]

Years ago when Veronica and I were starving college students, we traveled to Amsterdam with friends. The first morning we got up early and found a fifteen-dollar tour that included a channel boat ride through Amsterdam, stops at windmills, and a walk through the tulip fields—all for fifteen dollars.

We excitedly told everyone else, but one couple said, "We can't go."

"Why?" I wondered.

"It's too expensive."

Expensive? Okay, granted, it was fifteen dollars in the 80s, so in today's money that would be about … fifteen dollars. It's just fifteen dollars. It's not much now, and it wasn't much then.

She went on, "There are some things in life we're just not going to be able to do, and this is going to have to be one of them." Now understand this, I wasn't taking them cliff diving in Acapulco or swimming with the piranhas in the Amazon; this was a walk through tulip fields!

So the rest of us rode channel boats, climbed up inside windmills, and ate Dutch chocolate while walking through tulip fields painted every color of the rainbow—while the one couple stayed behind and read books in a dank, gray hotel room.

There's a life God meant you to live, but not everyone is living that life. We need to take an honest look at our lives and ask *what? why? who?* is keeping us in the gray days.

GARDENS OF COLOR

Let me tell you about one more garden. The Christ follower John tells us that Jesus was buried in a garden. But here's the really good

part: He did not remain buried in the garden. It was in the garden
that He got up. On a morning full of sunshine, He walked out of the
dark, gray stone cave and filled the world with light and life.

Jesus never liked to leave people in the dark, so He always gave
the same brief speech at funerals. You would think, as one of the
world's great orators, He would give more interesting speeches, more
elaborate speeches. His speech at funerals was always just two words
long:

"Get up!"

When the little girl lay lifeless on her bed, Jesus took her hand
and said, "Talitha—Get up!"

When the boy in Nain was being carried to his grave and Jesus
saw the tears of his mother, He stopped the processional and said,
"Get up!"

When his good friend Lazarus lay dead in a cave, Jesus cried,
"Get up!"

And on a sunny day in a garden full of color, on the edge of the
gritty city of Jerusalem, God himself said to His own Son, "Get up!"

Life is not meant to be lived in dark places; the days God gives
you on earth are not meant to be covered with gray clouds, so get
up and live.

Really, really live.

He will come down like rain.
Psalm 72:6[6]

Chapter 11

DÉSOLÉ

"None of them that trust in him shall be desolate."
Psalm 34:22[1]

While I was in Haiti recently, I said *désolé* often.

In French *désolé* means "sorry."

When I say, "I'm sorry" to people in America, they look at me a little funny and say, "It wasn't your fault." But growing up in Africa, *sorry* said it all. When someone was hurt, when someone was melancholy, you would simply say *sorry*.

To say sorry in Liberia is to say, "I empathize—I share your pain—I hurt because you hurt—you do not hurt alone."

Nobody should have to hurt alone.

In Malawi when someone is in sorrow, they are never left alone. When tragedy comes, the furniture is taken out of the house so that people can come in. They come and sit on the floor. They sit for hours. No one says anything; your presence says everything: *I'm sorry, and you are not alone in your sorrow.*

I don't think God meant for us to be alone when life really hurts; that's why I said *désolé* so many times in Haiti.

Our English word *desolate* comes from the French *désolé*. *Desolate* is a heavy word; we use it when we are deserted, abandoned, alone, or absent of joy. Maybe its most weighted meaning is "devoid of comfort."

That's why I said *désolé* in Haiti. I simply wanted the hurting people I met to know they were not alone in their pain.

As our team of doctors and nurses worked at field hospitals (literally on the grass in fields), at clinics, and at orphanages, I first wondered in what ways I could help. I'm a doctor—of philosophy— but that doesn't help when someone needs a leg set or a wound dressed.

But when I met a Haitian boy named Kevin, who had an amputated leg, without thinking much, the word *désolé* just came out. Haitians speak French (French Creole); he smiled and said, "*Merci.*"

Across the dirt road from the orphanage where we delivered food sat a pile of broken concrete that used to be a two-story home. I walked over to see if anyone was in the bedsheet tent in front of the pile of the rubble. A young woman in her twenties was living there. Her name is Rosetta. Her story hurt my heart. Rosetta and twenty other family members are sleeping in front of and behind their crumbled home. Some sleep between the crevices in the slabs of concrete. Two of her family are still buried in the rubble.

What do you say when you hear that? How much sorrow can one person take? The only words I really had were, *"Je suis très désolé"*—I am so very sorry.

As we drove through Port-au-Prince, a colorful Haitian bus pulled in front of us; in huge, bright letters on the bus were the words *Sorry My Friend.* The bus said it well. *Désolé mon ami*

Leaving Haiti, we stopped to deliver meds at a field hospital. As we came up to rows and rows of Red Cross tents that sheltered hundreds of recovering patients with amputations, crush wounds, and broken bones, I noticed that a teenage boy, probably nineteen, was laying alone on a bare mattress, under a tree that shaded him from the setting sun. Four large metal pins extruded through his skin as part of the external bone fixator that immobilized his tibia.

The field hospital was doing a superb job, but it felt strange that a patient with critical injuries was left alone under a tree. So I walked over and asked, *"Êtes vous d'accord?"* ("Are you okay?"). He said he was doing fine.

In spite of having the metal fixator protruding from his skin in four different places on his right leg, I could see that his leg and foot were intact. But a white bed sheet covered his left leg, and my heart sank as I thought that it was probably amputated like the hundreds of others all around us. Struggling to find the right words in French, I mustered the courage to ask him how his left leg was doing… He knew what I was thinking, so he pulled back the sheet with a big smile on his face and we both started to laugh; his left leg and foot were perfectly fine.

But he was still alone, so I sat down on the grass next to him and practiced my French for a while—and said *désolé mon ami.*

I HURT TOO

The day Damalise died, after the fire in the chapel, my wife Veronica and I went to the Mutahli family's home. All of the furniture was taken out of the Mutahlis' dimly lit house. Small rugs were scattered on the tiled floor. We slipped off our shoes and sat on the floor with their family and friends—in silence. They were there to simply sit with them on this darkest night of their lives. The women wept quietly; some would go outside to wail. The men sat somber.

The silence surprised me. I was reminded of the silence of God when life is bleak. The silence felt good. No one tried to talk. No one tried to say the really trite things we often say when life hurts. No one pretended to have simple answers.

The Malawians sit in silence with one another when life is dark to say, "We care about you, we love you, we are with you." They sit in silence to say, "When you hurt, I hurt too." They sit in silence to say, "The night may be dark, but you don't have to sit alone."

SHIVA

Tragedy has this interesting way of bringing people together, shaping a bond. It was good to watch the rescuers in Haiti work together; they came from Israel, South Africa, Taiwan, Turkey, Mexico, Los Angeles.

The Hebrew people have always known that it's good to come together when life really hurts. They call it *shiva* (which means seven, or sits of seven).

When there is death, the closest family members come together: the father and mother, brothers and sisters, sons and daughters, and spouses. They come together and sit. But they don't sit alone; all their friends and family come and sit with them. They sit until the healing begins. They sit because they want you to know you're not alone in your sorrow.

They sit together for seven days, and here's what I love about the seventh day—everyone in the community comes on the seventh day, and they walk with them around the block. The subtle message is, *You can begin to live again. We know you hurt, and we hurt with you, but you can heal over.*

That's why God gave us this thing we call the church, community. Because sometimes we just need someone with us in our affliction to say, *I'm sorry.*

God does that for us and in us too. Jesus talked about the Spirit of God as our Comforter. He is. He sits with you on every day that is difficult. He'll walk around the block if you need that, too.

ROSETTA'S TENT

Ten-year-old Deannzi greeted us with a bright smile as she stood in front of her broken home. She pointed us through the rubble to where we could find her aunt.

I was back in Haiti, two months after I met had Rosetta. I've had a tough time forgetting about Rosetta. I don't think life gets any worse than when you end up living on the dirt in front of your broken home full of sorrow.

Late one afternoon, as the hot Haitian sun went down and the air cooled, I stopped to visit Rosetta with Tom and Matt and Rich. She's still living on the dirt. I thought she might be, and I knew that when the rains come her bedsheet home will become a muddy pit, so I brought Rosetta a tent.

But as we put the tent together, it looked small. Target labeled it a "six-man" tent—it's not that big; I wished it was bigger.

Rosetta smiled. She was gracious and said *merci* a lot.

I sure wished the tent was bigger.

She said since the earthquake crumbled their home on January 12, no one from anywhere has stopped to give them anything. Deannzi's father asked if we had another tent; they were living under bedsheets too. We did, so we set up another tent for Deannzi's family. As we finished putting up the tents, Rosetta warmly thanked us again; I still wished the tent was bigger.

I guess I had wanted to do something bigger. The team of twenty-three from The Grove was a mile away building a new dorm for orphans; that felt big. The Grove is building a twelve-thousand-square-foot gym for African Bible College in Liberia; that feels big. This bright green tent, dwarfed by slabs of broken concrete piled high behind it, looked small.

The lime green "six-man" tent was the biggest one they had at Target, but I know I could have found a bigger one if I had just tried harder. I really wished I had looked harder for the biggest one I could buy. But I thought I was busy and didn't have time.

After we said good-bye to Rosetta, I told Tom I wished the tent was bigger. Tom said he thought the tent was good. He said, "It's better than the dirt that will turn to mud when the rains come, plus the brilliant green tent seemed to really brighten Rosetta's day."

He was right; it was good to see Rosetta smile.

I guess I say all this to remind all of us—remind me—that sometimes the world's troubles seem so daunting that we begin to believe that our efforts will be too small to matter, what we do is just a drop in the bucket. So at times we choose to do nothing—rather than something small.

Tom's words reminded me that God has a way of using our small efforts too. Because isn't it true that God uses one person to touch one life at a time?

So maybe on some days it's okay to do the small things that are good.

Because on some days, maybe God wants to sprinkle heaven just one drop at a time.

SWEET SORROW

She woke to find
Her dreams had faded ...
Her hope was all that held her high
Her heart was shattered
And the words no longer came,
No longer was she the same,
As she gazed upon that starry night
She knew he was gone ...

The moon enticed her
And so ...
The tears slowly molded to her tired face

They gently fell without a sound,
Much in liking as her silent heartbreak

She gazed,
Tired & Alone at that starry night,
That in her eyes shone

And in her gaze
She only found,
Memories of fond moments at his side

In that moment of pure sorrow,
She fell in love once more ...
As she gazed upon that starry sky,
As she recalled all those fond moments,
She fell in love with the full moon....
Once more again

She fell in love
She fell in love with hope....

In her sorrow she didn't hesitate
To fall in love with hope.[1]

Damaris P.

Chapter 12

TAKE HER BACK

Forgive my bad life; it's been a very bad life.
Psalm 25:11[1]

Shaun and Leslie were the all-LA couple. She was an executive with Gap, and he did promotion for movie studios; on top of this they loved God. They were good friends of mine and flew me out from Chicago to perform their wedding. So when Shaun called me nine months after they were married to say it was all falling apart, I was floored.

The story is painful. Leslie had begun going out for drinks and dancing after work with her coworkers. At a club she met a medical student who showed her more attention than she thought her husband did. She felt loved, and at the same time felt she was falling out of love with Shaun. A few weeks later she and the medical student began sleeping together.

In the midst of this, Leslie discovered she was pregnant. Confused and scared, she spilled everything out to Shaun.

After listening to every last painful detail, Shaun said something that I don't think I could ever say in a moment like that: "I forgive you—and I still love you."

But here's when it all really began to hurt. Leslie said, "I'm sorry, but I don't love you anymore; I'm in love with him."

And then when you think life could not hurt any worse, she said, "Shaun, I don't know if the baby is yours or his."

I honestly can't even bring myself to imagine the pain and the emotions that swept Shaun's body. But Shaun held on. He forgave her from the bottom of his heart, even when she was not asking him to. Over the ensuing weeks he just loved her. And took care of her. She wanted to leave, but he begged her to stay.

She did. And God worked a miracle in her heart. She fell in love with Shaun all over again.

And then Shaun called me. He said, "Palmer, she's told this man she has no feelings for him, but he still keeps calling. And now he's telling her he wants to see *his* new baby—he doesn't even know if it's his or mine. What should I do?"

I was so mad listening to Shaun I couldn't see straight. I said, "Shaun, I'll tell you what we need to do; we need to beat him down. I'll fly out from Chicago right now if you tell me to." Not very pastoral—maybe I should have said, "Let's pray for him"—but that's how I felt. He turned down my offer.

Eight months later Shaun and Leslie went to the hospital to have their new son. Shaun called me from the hospital room as soon as their son was born. It was a wonderful day, except when he called, he also told me that the creepy guy was standing in the hospital parking lot saying he wanted to see *his* son!

LOVE BITES

As sweet as the feeling of being in love is, the possibility always exists that those we love the deepest will hurt us the most.

People inflict some of life's deepest wounds. C. S. Lewis explains in *The Problem of Pain,* "The possibility of pain is inherent in the very existence of a world where souls can meet. When souls become wicked they will certainly use this possibility to hurt one another."[2] Just as surely as we will encounter physical pain, we also will be hurt by people we know and love.

I've honestly told Shaun that I don't know if I would be able to forgive if I were in his shoes. I'm just being straight with you. It all seems too painful. And for the most part, I think many of us would far prefer to remain bitter than give someone who has wounded us the satisfaction of forgiveness.

But bitterness eats a hole on the inside; it has the power to lock us in misery. Bitterness turns into depression. It holds us captive to the treatment of others. People who linger in bitterness become cynical, mean, angry—and they wear animosity on their sleeve.

Angry people become isolated people. Our anger affects and infects everyone around us. As it destroys us, it destroys relationships with those we care about most. Anne Lamott says that harboring bitterness and unforgiveness is "like drinking rat poison and then waiting for the rat to die."[3]

THE PIT STINKS

Bitter people lose their beauty. And maybe worst of all, bitter people struggle to stay close to God. Angry people are usually also angry at God, blaming Him for their pain. Their relationships with God and others suffers as their lives become defined by bitterness, stuck in a pit of unforgiveness.

The pit stinks. One Christmas Eve, Bob Schoff of Des Moines spent hours upside down in the worst pit possible: a clogged septic tank. Bob had dug a two-foot by two-foot hole three feet deep to the top of his tank. He slipped down the hole and braced himself with his left hand and reached into the tank's opening with his right. While attempting to dislodge a wad of toilet paper from the drain into the tank, Bob's left hand slipped, sending him headfirst into the tank. His body wedged neatly into the hole, leaving his head dangling just inches above the raw mess. His arms were pinned to his side, Superman-like, and his feet stuck straight up in the air. Bob says his day in the pit was the worst Christmas Eve of his life. A bit of an understatement, I would say.[4]

This is where we end up when we refuse to forgive.

David resented God for allowing his son to die, and his soul slipped into a pit. In his state of resentment and anger toward God he says,

> I'm a black hole in oblivion.
> You've dropped me into a bottomless pit.[5]

Joseph of the Old Testament ended up in this pit of unforgiveness. His brothers were jealous, so they literally dug a hole for him to die in.

God got him out, but he harbored bitterness for years. He tried so hard to hold on to his anger when he saw them again, but he couldn't. He wanted out of the pit so he finally let go. He forgave. He loved again.

IT'S WORTH THE RISK

Guys, have you ever gazed long and deep into the eyes of a beautiful girl and dug inside for the courage to say, "I love you!"? It's a risk, a huge risk. Because there's always the possibility that she will smile and say, "That's really nice." Then keep eating her chicken Parmesan. That can really happen. And not that I'm saying it's happened to me.

My sophomore year in college, I met Veronica. She had long dark hair, was tall and thin and gorgeous. She looked like she stepped out of *Vogue*. The moment I met her I knew she was it. She had my heart. I was slain. I was in a love coma. I walked like a zombie back to the dorm and told my friend Joel, "I just met the girl I'm going to marry." He thought I was nuts. I was.

I finally mustered the courage to ask her out. I knew I needed to move quickly before some loser beat me to it. I found her by the mailboxes after dinner the first week of the semester, and as casually as I could, I mumbled, "Would you want to go to Knott's Berry Farm with me this Friday night?"

Now understand, I was the skinny, insecure missionary kid from Africa, and she was *the* hot girl on campus—from Vegas. So I wasn't terribly surprised when she said, "Ah, I can't. I'm supposed to babysit this weekend."

Now a lesser man would have slinked away with his tail between his legs, because she sure didn't leave the door open with, "But Saturday works, or next weekend works." Nothing.

But I knew she was it. So out of nowhere—on the fly—I pulled out, "Forget about Knott's, how about Disneyland?" as though I never heard the whole lame babysitting thing.

Jackpot! I had no idea she was a Disneyland freak. There was no place in the world she would rather be. Who knew? But it was a masterful move.

"I'll get out of the babysitting," she blurted out excitedly.

We kissed on the Matterhorn. Two years later she married me.

You see, with the risk comes the possibility of great reward. When you love somebody, there's always the beautiful possibility that they will love you back.

God took this risk when He sent His Son. He said, "Because I love you so much, I will let my own Son die so that you may live. All you have to do is love me back."

That's the risk.

Love is like that. You put your heart on the line. You lay it all out and make yourself vulnerable to someone else. But love is worth this risk of pain because love also holds life's most beautiful experiences. When somebody loves you back, you float. You can't eat. Nothing else matters. And nothing's sweeter.

HOW TO REALLY LOVE

The Bible holds a story about forgiveness of epic proportions. The man of God Hosea had a wife named Gomer, who strayed from him. She was not just unfaithful in the marriage; she abandoned her husband and children and sold her body as a prostitute. The pain would seem unbearable. I can't think of greater humiliation or loss or betrayal.

But here's what God told Hosea to do: *Get her back*. So Hosea went down to the seedy end of town where prostitutes stood on display and paid to have his own wife come home with him. He forgave her. He held none of her wrong against her. He loved her again.

Forgiving a wrong is one of life's most beautiful acts of love. The beauty of forgiveness comes in the fact that true forgiveness is often unmerited.

But know this about forgiveness: It almost always comes with a price. The price often is pride, your pride, because you let the offender go free without paying a price. You see, we want vengeance. We want to get even. We want the one who has hurt us to feel our pain—even if it's just the pain we can wield with unforgiveness. But if you have any hope of healing, you have to forgive.

You must let go.

WHO NEEDS FORGIVENESS ANYWAY?

Forgive the ones who ask you to forgive. One of life's more beautiful moments is when someone you love comes to ask for forgiveness. Forgive them.

Forgive those who don't even know they have wounded you. Life will have moments when we find a careless word or action brutally offensive. Some have absolutely no idea their actions hurt you so badly. Everything in us wants to confront their boorish behavior. But let it go.

And forgive the ones who will never ask forgiveness. If you don't, you will be the one carrying the baggage of pain. Sometimes we harbor unforgiveness to remember the wound, hoping to make the other person hurt too. But unforgiveness will wear you out and eat you up. It will turn life dark and gray.

BRIGHTER

Sometimes forgiveness is the only way out of darkness. A divorce, for example, can put a person in the pit of resentment and enmity for years, even decades. The anger we feel toward another person can become obsessive. It can darken your entire countenance, like ominous thunderclouds on a gloomy day. The lights go out. We become lost.

That is why I say there is so much freedom in forgiveness. We don't just forgive others for what it does for them; we forgive so that we can get out of the pit of unforgiveness and be cut free from the weight of animosity, revenge, and rage. Life weighs less when we have figured out that forgiving is good.

The next few days were tense as Shaun and Leslie waited for the DNA results. Regardless of the outcome, Shaun promised Leslie that his love for her would never change.

Finally, the results came back—the baby was Shaun's, without a doubt.

Shaun and Leslie freely share their story with couples. They particularly want couples who are in the midst of a crumbling marriage to know there is hope. Leslie unequivocally says it was because of Shaun's unconditional forgiveness and unchanging love that their marriage, darkened by sin, was saved.

They now have five beautiful children, they're still in love, and Shaun and Leslie have started a church on the beach in Southern California—where the sun shines bright.

I'M SORRY

Verse 1
How can you look at me the same way
With what I did to you?
How can you even talk to me,
With what I did to you?
I would be devastated,
If you,
Found out and knew … the truth.
So I'm saying ahead of time,
Sorry to you.

Verse 2
How can you love me,
When you see that guilt in my eyes?
How can you laugh with me,
When you see my phony smile?
I don't want to lose you even,
If I,
Stray from the truth.
So I'm saying ahead of time,
Sorry to you.

Bridge
Oh I'm sorry,

Please forgive me.
I didn't mean to,
Betray you.
How could I ever,
Make it better?
Please just hear me out,
And listen now.

Oh, I'm sorry,
Yes, I'm sorry.
I hope you still love me,
Because I still ...
Love you.[6]

C.A.M.

Chapter 13

HEAL OVER

He heals the brokenhearted and binds up their wounds.
Psalm 147:3

The first day our team of doctors and nurses from The Grove arrived in Barahona, near the Haiti–Dominican border, they were assigned to meet a pair of U.S. military Black Hawk helicopters ferrying in children who had been critically injured in the tragic earthquake.

Running under helicopter blades, Dr. John Hodgson and the team carried out eleven boys and girls on stretchers. It looked like a scene out of *M*A*S*H* or *The Hurt Locker*. Five had amputations, six had broken legs and arms; several had multiple fractures. Others had gaping wounds. None had been washed or cleaned since their concrete homes came crashing down on their fragile lives.

When I first saw the kids, my initial thought was, *Will they ever heal over?* The tragedy and trauma all seemed too much for one child to bear. I felt a bit of anger, maybe even at God; life is not supposed to hurt this much.

But life gets like that for just about all of us. It may not have happened when you were seven, but pain will come. Like the darkness of night that always snuffs out the beauty of a spring day, the times of sorrow will cover all of us.

But here's what I want you to know right here, right now: God can't sleep.

The ancient prophet Obadiah wrote about our sleepless God. He wrote to the Hebrew people when their lives were stolen away in Babylonian exile. At first glance, when you read Obadiah, it appears that his words are warnings of coming judgment on Edom, but that's not his message at all. Obadiah's words are words of hope. He encourages Israel, saying, *There will be justice; something good will come out of this very bad thing Edom has done to you.*

The story of Edom is a story of bitterness. It began with hatred between twin brothers. The people of Edom were descendants of Esau, who hated his brother, Jacob.

First, Jacob conned Esau out of his inheritance with a bowl of soup; and then Jacob used another bowl of soup to steal Esau's blessing from their dying father, Isaac.[1] Jacob must have been a pretty good cook, like Rachael Ray or Emeril.

Esau moved east. His family grew into a people named *Edom,* "red," like the color of his hair. Edom sat east of the Jordan, east of Israel, east of God. The animosity between Edom and Israel never died; it grew.

Tensions heightened when Edom would not allow Israel to pass through their red-dirt land on their way to the Promised Land. Then, in Israel's great hour of need, when enemies are about to crash down the gates of Jerusalem, the Edomites refuse to lift a hand to help. And worse, to rub salt in the open wound, they join the invading enemy![2]

Edom sides with Babylon!

Obadiah says to Edom, "Because of the violence against your brother Jacob, you will be covered with shame; you will be destroyed forever."[3]

YOU CAN'T HEAL OVER ON YOUR OWN

Obadiah warns the Edomites that God "will bring you down … [because] you stood aloof."[4] When we think we can do it all on our own, God is annoyed. And the thing we have a very hard time doing on our own is healing over.

So many people try to do this life on their own, without God. It never goes well like that. It's like trying to build a house with a lot of sand and not enough steel.

That was the problem in Haiti. Houses were built with too much sand and not enough steel. Sand is cheap, so because of poverty, when many Haitians built their cement-block homes, they used more sand than they should have in their mortar mix. And because steel is expensive, they didn't use enough steel in the columns and ring beams. So when the ground quaked, homes crumbled; there was too much sand and not enough steel.

It was a tragedy of poverty.

In our own poverty of spirit, we try to build lives this way:

We build marriages with too much anger and not enough
love … and they crumble.
We build reputations on too much pride and not enough
humility … and they crumble.
We build families on too much busyness and not enough
time … and they crumble.
We build friendships on too much criticism and not
enough grace … and they crumble.

LOOK UP

Pain has its own way of pointing us back to God; it makes us look up.

I was unloading medical supplies at a field hospital in Haiti when
the ground began to shake. Two of our doctors had just walked into
the small makeshift operating theatre—a yellow schoolhouse built out
of concrete! I turned just in time to see them sprint out the door, fly
off the four-foot-high porch, and land safely on the shaking ground.

It was an aftershock.

In one voice a cry of panic rose from the hundreds of healing
Haitians under tents.

Then right in front of me, an older, gray-haired Haitian gentleman raised his arms and looked toward heaven and shouted out,
"Mon Dieu, *mon Dieu.*" My God, *my God.*

Life is kind of like that; affliction makes us look up. Suffering
reminds us to depend on Him, not ourselves.

The eleven kids were taken to a small Dominican clinic where our team worked frantically to make them comfortable. The first thing the team did was wash each child. They filled bucket after bucket with the dirt and grime they washed off the children's bodies and from their hair.

The children were beautiful.

Each child was carefully laid in a bed with crisp sheets and clothed in new hospital gowns.

They started to smile.

More doctors and nurses began to pour in that night from places across America—enough medical staff to give each child attention twenty-four hours a day.

The kids started to heal.

When I walked through the doors of the clinic on the third day, eight-year-old Luciano was playing soccer. Two weeks earlier Luciano was playing soccer on a small field near his home when the earthquake struck. A two-story building next to the field collapsed on Luciano, crushing his right arm. To save him from the spread of gangrene, doctors amputated his arm high at the shoulder.

So when I walked in the clinic, I did a double take; a boy with fresh wounds and one arm was playing soccer with a purple inflated surgical glove. I took him on. He was good. We laughed.

I walked away a little baffled. How can he laugh? He's left to go through life with one arm, and he's laughing. He's still in pain from the traumatic amputation, and he's laughing.

He's healing over.

Maybe we can learn from that.

If Luciano can laugh again—so can you.

HEAL OVER

Healing begins in our places of pain; it's a strange thing, but it's true.

Do you see how in exile, in Babylon, Israel began to heal with God?

If there's good in pain, maybe it's that it causes us, forces us, to stretch out our hands for God to grab on. And maybe if we are never in the places of exile and slavery, we will never realize our need for God.

By the rivers of Babylon, Israel began to heal over.

Sometimes the scars remain, the tears still form, but you can heal over.

Jesus is very good at healing over. He heals wounds, sorrow, heartache, brokenness, sadness, marriages, families, love. You see, Jesus suffered too. He was there. He felt the pain and the shame and the heartbreak that you do. He knows how you feel.

After watching Luciano kick around a purple surgical glove and laugh, I thought, *If a boy with one arm can play soccer with a balloon made from a purple surgical glove and laugh, then so can I. So can you.*

My final morning in Barahona, I poked my head into the clinic to say good-bye to the kids. They were singing. Kevin, who now only had one leg, was singing. Luciano was singing. Bolivna with the broken femur was singing. Marthias, whose leg was amputated below the knee, was singing. All the children were singing.

When Israel was crying in the desert under Babylonian captivity, the psalmist asked, "How can we sing?"[5] the Babylonians have sucked the music out of our lives.

But if you really believe God can heal you over, you can sing.

The cross is where exile ends and healing begins. Jesus said to His friends, "Remember my pain, my broken body. And I bled, a lot—and died. But don't just remember the pain, remember this most, I rose again!"[6]

I was recently back in Barahona, weeks after the quake. The children's wounds that replaced their amputated limbs had healed over. Five of the eleven returned home with their families, back to Haiti.

It's time for you to heal over too.

DEAR STORM

help me please
mix with my tears
and wash away everything
my pain, fears and sorrow
let it flow out with the rain

drown out the noise of my cries with thunder
let the lightning keep me company, however briefly it stays

i'm used to it

i usually dance alone

without a partner or a friend
let me dance with you.

clouds hover over and make my world dark
i've lost my sunshine anyway
why not make it a reality?

surround me in darkness
so black no one can see me

for i am so ugly when i cry

and after the rain ceases and i am dry and warm
when i am alone in silence without the thunder
the lightning no longer appears, and i
   will remember its short visits
when i am too tired from dancing
and when the wind calms and the world is still

the clouds will disappear and the sun will shine again
leaving a colorful rainbow
i will be strong
and i will find another light in my life
and i will look around to see the flowers

they have matured and blossomed
just like i have
they survived the storm and still stand strong

just like i am
and mostly, they are beautiful
just like me[7]

Callie Hansen
(TheatreFreak)

Chapter 14

HOLD ON

He reached down from on high and took hold of me.
Psalm 18:16

Magnus Beah was a member of the faculty at African Bible College, where I taught in Liberia. He was one of many good friends I left behind when my wife, Veronica, and I escaped Liberia at the outset of the country's violent civil war. Soon after we left, Charles Taylor's rebel soldiers overran our city. Sensing his life was in danger, Magnus slipped across the border one night to neighboring Guinea, then on to his native Sierra Leone.

His refuge was short-lived. Under the name Revolutionary United Front (RUF), a rebel army formed in Sierra Leone to export diamonds. The rebels controlled the jungles and the mines but now wanted the capital city of Freetown. As they advanced on the capital city, they went on a bloody, drug-induced rampage. To instill terror and fear, the RUF began hacking off the arms of men, women, and children. In a hideous jest, the RUF soldiers (many of whom were boy soldiers), would ask before hacking off an arm, "Do you want it long sleeve or short sleeve?" Tens of thousands of Sierra Leoneans had their arms cut off in this way. Such inhumanity is among the worst atrocities committed upon the landscape of Africa's bloody civil wars.

In a surprising assault, the RUF rebels scattered the government troops and overran Freetown. They quickly established control of large sectors of the city, and Magnus, along with thousands of others, was trapped behind rebel lines. His wife was able to slip out to safety as the rebels took control, but Magnus and his son remained trapped. For days they hid quietly in their home, hoping to remain undetected.

When food ran out and they grew more certain of being discovered, Magnus decided to make a run for the government-controlled sector of the city. At dusk, just as the sun set, Magnus and his son began to move from alley to alley. They crawled behind hedges, took cover behind houses, and sprinted across deserted streets. But with less than half a mile to go and the government checkpoint within sight, an RUF soldier caught a glimpse of them and immediately began shouting, "Traitor, traitor!" as he sprinted toward them.

In most African wars you would fear an AK-47 blast or a machete, but this rebel's weapon of choice was a hacksaw, the preferred tool for cutting off an arm. Magnus grabbed his eight-year-old son's hand and began to sprint. The checkpoint was only several hundred yards away, but the rebel with the hacksaw was bearing down hard on them.

IN HIS GRIP

It feels good when someone holds you tight.

In many ways, this is a picture of the strong and loving grip of our heavenly Father. He holds His children tightly. In life's most difficult situations, He holds on. His grip never loosens. He will never leave you behind or let go of your hand. And He promises to pull you through.

God is famous for His grip. Jesus said, "My sheep listen to my voice; I know them, and they follow me. I give them eternal life, and they shall never perish; no one can snatch them out of my hand."[1]

I love the Latin phrase that theologians use to speak of the mighty hand of God: *Manus Dei*. I can't think of a better feeling than knowing God's massive hand is on your life. I want to remind you today that when life is troubled, God holds on.

I always wanted hands large enough to palm a basketball. Before high school basketball games, my buddies and I would wrap duct tape backward around several fingers, then palm a ball as we walked out of the locker room and onto the court. We thought the girls were impressed.

The Bible often speaks about the great hand of God. God told the ancient prophet Isaiah, "I will uphold you with my righteous right hand."[2] Jabez asked God, "Let your hand be with me."[3] And David claimed, "Your right hand will hold me fast."[4]

When I picture Jesus, I see Him with strong hands. We often forget that Jesus was a construction worker. Often we picture Him with kids in His lap or having hot chocolate and marshmallows with the retirees. That's just not who He was. He is a strong Savior.

He reached down with the Manus Dei and held up sinking Peter. He grabbed the tables in front of God's house and threw them across the courtyard. He extended the Manus Dei to the lame man and lifted him up. And He held on to the nails in the cross to rescue me.

Jesus so often reached out His hand and showed mercy with His touch. When a little girl lay dead on her bed, He took her by the hand and said, "Get up." When the blind man came to Him for help, with mud on his fingertips, He touched his eyes—and the man could see. When the lepers came begging for Jesus to make them clean, He touched the untouchables. And the bleeding woman was made well when she reached out to touch the Christ.

Do you know that, as humans, we thrive on touch? Research has shown that when patients in the hospital are touched by people who care, they heal more quickly. So now when doctors are taught bedside manners, they're told to put their hand on the patient's arm or knee because their touch literally heals. Chemically, things happen in our bodies; we release endorphins, our blood pressure lowers. God made us to long for touch.

DESPERATE

The great problem in our suffering is that we give up. We don't believe we can take the pain. So we quit. We let go and give up. But quitting rarely solves anything.

Kelly's father, Frank, had left me a message, "Kelly is desperate—could you please stop by and see her and tell her not to give up? I think she listens to you."

I called Frank back on my way home that evening but only got his voice mail. I left him a message back; I didn't know where she lived and said I would call in the morning.

At six-thirty Friday morning, Kelly's husband, Allen, kissed her good-bye. She seemed to be doing better. Their marriage had been on the rocks. She had lost her job. She struggled with addiction and had been in and out of rehab. But her parents loved her, Allen had not given up on her, and she had three beautiful kids.

Kelly lay in bed for a while after Allen left. Then at seven that morning, she took a gun out of Allen's closet and shot herself in the head. Her twelve-year-old daughter, ten-year-old son, and seven-year-old daughter were in the next room.

I was so mad at myself. I don't know if I've ever felt like such a failure as a pastor. Why didn't I try harder to find Kelly? Why didn't I call Frank back sooner? Why didn't I notice a long time ago that Kelly really, really hurt? She sat on the second row in our church. Why didn't I see the pain? Why didn't I help stop the agony?

Kelly gave up. She gave up on her marriage. She gave up on God. She gave up on life. She couldn't hold on any anymore.

If life aches to the gut right now, I know you want to give up on God. I know you want to throw your religion out the window because you just can't take the pain anymore.

Just about everyone hits that wall. The ancient man of God Job ended up in that place. His friends had run out of words to comfort him in his anguish. His wife had had enough so she said, "Curse God and die!"[5]

But let me tell you what I wanted to tell Kelly: Hold on! Don't give up. God holds on to you and will get you through this. Darkness is not the end.

He really is the God who never lets go. We doubt His presence and love. But I want you to know He's the *wounded healer*. He's walked the path of pain Himself, and now He sits with you in your anguish.

Hold on because He's holding on to you.

DON'T LET GO

I realize I was scarred when I was young, and I'm sure that's the reason why people who quit really bother me.

I had known Birdie for almost ten years. She and I both grew up in the jungles of Liberia, and we were both twins. She was American, according to her passport, but she was Liberian to the core. Her senior year in high school, her class left for a weekend on the beach in Côte d'Ivoire. She had grown up only several hundred yards from the Atlantic, but like many Liberians, Birdie never learned to swim well.

She waded out waist deep into the ocean to visit with her friends when a swell took her off her feet, and the riptide swept her away from shore. An American teacher immediately dove in and swam toward Birdie. He reached her, but she was desperate and tired. He fought to keep her up and tried his best to pull her back.

The continental shelf drops steeply off the West African coast and creates treacherous rip currents. The teacher and student were being pulled farther out to sea. She was getting heavier, and he was exhausted.

He

let

go....

I laid in bed many nights after that day feeling rage toward that teacher. Furious. Spitting mad. How could you let go? You can't let go! Why would you give up on Birdie?

I made a promise to myself then—I would never quit on anybody. No matter what. I would never give up on anyone who needed me. I try to live that way. I think that's how God wants it. That we live knowing there's always hope, that we never give up. If that young American teacher had known the African currents better, he would have known they always bring you back. They are circular. If you just tread water, the same vicious current that swept you out will bring you right back to shore.

Don't ever quit. Don't give up. Don't let go. Hold on. Live your life full of hope.

Jesus never gave up on anyone. He didn't give up on Lazarus. He wouldn't leave the adulterous woman. He refused to let go of Peter when the waves were pulling him under, not even to teach him a lesson. And He'll never give up on you and me.

I've learned in life that people usually find it easier to quit than to hold on and persevere. I don't think Christians should quit anything easily. Don't quit your golf lessons. Don't quit rehab. Don't quit on your friendships. Don't quit going to church. Don't let your kids quit football when the practice is too tough and the coach yells at them. Let the world quit. Be known for your tenacity because you belong to the God of great hope.

Hold on. God wants to lead you somewhere wonderful. I'm not making that up. He did that for people like the Jews of the Bible, and He'll do that for you.

Mandy had been a part of my college ministry for a number of years. She became a close friend of my wife. She even helped raise my sons—she was their favorite sitter. But then college was over, the years were passing quickly, and she still was not married.

Mandy didn't just want to get married; she wanted kids! Maybe that's one of the reasons guys never stayed around long.

Looking for love, she sank in and out of abusive relationships.

She was pushing thirty and began feeling like this singleness would last a lifetime. Depression set in. She started seeing a psychiatrist who put her on medication. The pills made her worse.

Vomiting and suicidal, she called Veronica. Veronica stayed with her and simply told her to hold on. Hold on because God loved her so much and had a beautiful future for her.

I called her psychologist, got him out of bed, and told him to get her off his drugs. I was furious. She didn't need pills; she needed love.

Mandy held on. Two years later she fell in love with a young pastor ... and he fell in love with her. Today she has two tiny people of her own, holding on to her.

Having played soccer with Magnus many times, I can attest to his strength and speed, but this sprint of a lifetime was uphill, and the weight of his son in tow was slowing him down.

The rebel was gaining. Recalling the moment, Magnus said, "I could hear his feet pounding the pavement as he closed the distance between us. Now close enough for me to hear his heavy breathing. I glanced back, and he was just yards behind me. My lungs were burning and my legs felt so heavy."

As Magnus shared his story, he paused to say, "Palmer, there was one thing I knew would never happen: I would never let go of my son!"

No matter how heavy or how much his son slowed him down, the father would never let go—never, no matter what: "I held on more tightly than I've held on to anything in my life and just kept running."

As Magnus crested the hill, the checkpoint was now just fifty yards away. Government soldiers behind sandbags aimed their guns past Magnus and at the rebel with the hacksaw. Magnus glanced back one more time. The rebel was slowing. He could not keep up with the running father. His motivation to cut off an arm did not equal the motivation of a father to save his son.

SAVE ME, PLEASE

I'm slipping.
I'm falling.
I'm stumbling down.
As I ponder the intensity of my impact with ground.
Why can't I stay up?
Why do I fall?
When I hit rock bottom will it hurt like before?
Every time I screw up
Every time I fail.
I can't climb this mountain.
This hill.
Keep telling yourself:
I'm not good enough
Or
Strong enough
And it won't hurt so bad
Won't hurt when others see you fail.
I'm sinking.
I'm floundering.
Down into the deep.
Gasping and choking the further I sink.
Why can't I float?
Why can't I swim?

Will someone come to my rescue?

Or am I all alone?

Alone in this world.

All by myself.

Here I am.

Nothing but You.

Only You can save me from myself.

So here I am!

Come to my side.

I need a protector

A Savior

A friend

One who will show me the Way.

The way back to You.[6]

MERCI

Chapter 15

DAYLIGHT

God turns my darkness into light.
Psalm 18:28

Hope is as necessary to the soul as the air we breathe. And Jesus Christ is the hope of the world. He holds out hope for everyone. He promises hope for those who have fallen into debt or are between jobs. Hope waits for blended families. Hope is for the overwhelmed student. Hope is there for the betrayed spouse. Hope waits for wanderers who need to come home.

Hope waits for all of us. Our hope is both present and future. Hope is for the dark days as well as the bright days, the gray days of winter, and the sunny days of summer. Hope waits for you.

DON'T EVER GIVE UP
Quitting is the antithesis of hope. Don't live that way.

I went to visit Craig today. Five weeks ago Craig was T-boned by a Chevy Avalanche driven by a drunk driver. The first paramedics on the scene radioed to the responding police officers that they would be investigating a fatality. But Craig's still alive ... and doing fantastic! His skull was fractured, his neck broken, ribs shattered, and his femur broken in two. But there is hope. Craig will walk again in just a few days. I'm sure of that, because he's a New Jersey native and a Yankee fan! Those guys always believe they will win. He's as upbeat as a kid at Disneyland. I think we should all live that way.

I saw a bumper sticker a while ago that read: "Rehab is for quitters." What does that mean? Hope is why we go to rehab. Hope is why we have babies. Hope is why we spend so much to send our kids to college. Hope is why we have counselors. Hope is why we go to church. Hope is why God sent His only Son, that whoever believes in Him will have life eternal. That's the best of all the hopes in the world.[1]

BTW: Craig has healed up beautifully.

HOPE CHANGES DARK LIVES

I've spent quite a bit of time in Latin American cities, but walking the streets of Havana for the first time was different, very different. At first I couldn't understand why Havana felt so odd. I thought maybe it was the long lines of people outside small shops all over the city, hoping to buy sugar or cabbage. Or was it the centuries-old architecture that sets Havana apart from other cities—beautiful, ornate Spanish construction that still looks amazing despite the fact that not a building in the city appears to have been painted for the past forty years? Then it hit me. It was the eyes. As I looked into the eyes of the Cuban people, I saw nothing. Their eyes were dull, vacant, and hollow. Joy was absent. Hopelessness was everywhere. Forty years of political, social, and spiritual oppression had taken its toll on the Cuban people. Their joy had been smothered. Their future seemed to hold so little, confined as they were to a communist island nation and doomed to a life of poverty and oppression.

The evening of that first day in Havana, however, we attended a church service. When I walked through the doors of the church, I was struck full in the face by something bright and alive. I realized in a moment it was the hope-filled eyes of Cuban Christians. The contrast was striking. In spite of living under the same cloud of oppression as those on the streets of Havana, hope was bright in the eyes of these Christians. I was reminded that God fills the dreariest lives with hope!

A THEOLOGY OF HOPE

You can't make yourself hope. Hope is a gift given by God. Hope gets us past the bitterness, through the depression, and on to new life. When pain turns life dark, know that there's hope in the light of Christ, even after the lights have been turned off.

Not too many of us think much about hope, so we lack an adequate theology or understanding of hope. Peter the Christ follower reminds us that we have a living hope. The world offers no such hope. Physicians only postpone the inevitable. Money is nice, but we all know it can't buy life. God is the only source of eternal hope!

Scripture speaks of our hope in several ways.

Hope as the Source of Joy

I've read that on average, children laugh three hundred times a day. Adults, on the other hand, laugh about fifteen times a day. What happens!? Why do we become such cranky, joyless people?

I grew up around a *Christian* woman whose name I still don't know because my friends and I only knew her as "Crabby Guts." Not very kind, but that's who she was. She was crabby about everything. Have you known people like that? Their life becomes a joy-vacuum. They have the ability to suck the life out of anything positive. I'll be honest; Christians need to stay (at least) over one hundred laughs a day because God fills the dreary soul with joy. He makes everything beautiful. The psalmist writes, "This is the day the LORD has made; let us rejoice and be glad in it."[2]

The Christian will always see life differently than the nonbeliever does. Joy is at our core, at the center of who we are. Pain is on the periphery. So when life hurts, we look inward and find the God-given hope, peace, and joy on which our life is centered.

Conversely, those who do not know the Christ have lives centered on pain. Theirs is a constant search outward, seeking happiness and fulfillment. It's a hollow life, void of joy and absent of meaning.

Live Optimistically and Full of Hope

Pessimistic people really bother me. I sometimes jokingly call one of my friends a *Prophet of Doom*. He doesn't think I'm funny. But if you consistently see the glass half empty and the sky falling, then that's who you are. When God is on our side, we have no reason to live pessimistically. Grab God's moments of impossible opportunity, and live defiantly against the odds.

The life of following after God is an adventure. Settle for nothing less.

This past Sunday, Mother's Day, is a Sunday I'll never forget.

At the end of each of our three services, we invited people to walk up on stage and take home the pictures of children who had no mothers and sponsor them: kids from Haiti, Liberia, and Malawi.

We hung a hundred profiles over the stage. The most kids we had ever had sponsored for Children of the Nations (COTN) in one Sunday was twenty-five. This would be four times that many. I thought we might be able to pull it off, but I wasn't sure.

We had received one hundred thirty-two profiles, but I thought if we had one hundred kids sponsored in one day, that would be amazing—and to be honest I wasn't quite sure one hundred thirty-two kids could be sponsored in one day, so I told my staff to leave thirty-two kids in a box. Yes, I was hedging—plus, I reasoned, we'd run out of room on our wire clotheslines … not that we couldn't have strung one more wire.

The idea was that on Mother's Day, children without mothers would be found and loved by families at The Grove.

That Sunday I told the people at The Grove that, if all the profiles were not gone by the end of the morning, the kids would still be hanging there next Sunday. And if every child was not adopted by a sponsor by the end of next Sunday, they would be hanging there the Sunday after that. "In fact," I said, "the pictures of these one hundred orphans will stay at the front of our auditorium until every child is taken home."

At the close of the eight o'clock service, twenty-eight kids were taken home. We were all thrilled. I was hopeful; I thought maybe by the end of the third service, they might all find a home.

But when we invited people up during the nine-thirty service, the stage was flooded. It seemed like every family present came to take a child home. People were practically grabbing profiles out of one another's hands. When the stage cleared, seventy more kids were sponsored! Just two profiles still hung there. They looked lonely.

Eric must have thought the same thing, because he ran down the aisle from the back row, jumped on stage, and grabbed the last two.

I loved the applause.

Now we had one more service, but the wire clotheslines were empty. Fortunately (due to my lack of optimism and faith!) we still had thirty-two profiles left in a box. We hung them for the third service, and they were gone in a heartbeat.

Jesus' brother James said, "True religion is to love widows and orphans."[3] If you live that way, thank you. Your religion really is true.

Take the impossible opportunities. Live optimistically and full of hope.

Hope for God to Use Your Pain

In the midst of his personal affliction, Paul the Christ follower wrote, "Praise be to the God and Father of our Lord Jesus Christ, the Father of compassion and the God of all comfort, who comforts us in all our troubles, so that we can comfort those in any trouble with the comfort we ourselves have received from God."[4]

As much as we don't like pain, we must realize that God can and will use our afflictions. Our pain often enables us to better minister to others who hurt. And many times God will directly use our wounds to change the lives of others.

I have not seen this truth lived out more clearly than when I traveled to Danané, Côte d'Ivoire, a town near the Liberian border, to minister to and encourage Liberian refugees who had fled their country's civil war. I had previously taught at African Bible College in Liberia, and when my former students learned I was coming, they gathered from all around to come spend time with me. One such student was Pastor Sam Weah.

When I asked Sam about his ministry in Liberia, he asked if he could show me his back. Taking off his shirt, he turned to show me dozens of gaping wounds. Sam went on to tell me the story of his stripes.

A couple of weeks earlier, he had returned to Liberia from Côte d'Ivoire with money for his ministry. The young rebel soldiers who controlled the border knew he was returning with money, so to have an excuse to rob him, they charged him with spying for the Liberian government, stripped him to his underwear, and for three days beat and whipped him with electrical cords. When they finally released him, his back was raw meat.

The third day after Sam's release was a Wednesday. He got up, dressed himself for the first time since coming home, picked up his Bible, and gingerly walked the five miles back to where he had been imprisoned. When the rebel soldiers saw him coming, they began to shout at him, saying, "What are you doing here? We have already released you." Sam replied, "Don't you know today is Wednesday? You know that every Wednesday I come here to lead the guards in prayer and Bible study."

Sam had been leading a Bible study at the border post every week since the war started, and he was not going stop ministering there just because they had imprisoned and beat him. So Sam said, "Call the guards together; it's time to pray." They began the service with singing, and they sang louder than ever before. And the one who just days before had mercilessly beat him read the Bible with him. Before Sam left that afternoon, almost a dozen men prayed with Sam to receive Jesus Christ as their Lord and Savior.

God can use your affliction for good. God does not cause pain, but He does use life's most hurtful experiences to change lives around us. So how is God trying to use your pain? Are you giving Him the opportunity to use your affliction for His kingdom? Have you returned to the place or to the people who caused your pain to see if God wants to use you to change others?

Hope that God Will Change You

Affliction proves and improves us. Affliction changes us forever. Pain can embitter us, scar us to the point that we become forever hostile people. Or God can use our pain to make us more beautiful vessels.

God shapes our character through pain. God uses what we don't like for good. Pain to the soul of those who suffer is like adrenaline to the body of the frightened. Our spiritual awareness heightens; we focus more clearly on God. In desperation we realize we need Him more than ever and can't do life on our own.

Hope for Heaven

The psalmist David wrote about heaven. He described his hope that "goodness and mercy shall follow me all the days of my life: and I will dwell in the house of the LORD forever."[5]

But most of us don't think much or talk much about heaven. It's not that we don't want to go to heaven; we just don't want to go today.

And maybe we're not excited about heaven because we don't know much about heaven. Let me impress you with a few images of heaven that I believe will capture your heart and mind. And I'll preface what I write with this: Whatever good I say about heaven is not enough; it's too small, too insignificant, too less-than-wonderful.

I'm fully convinced that God gives us snapshots of heaven in the world we live in right now.

We get a glimpse of heaven in every hug from our kids. Rain on a sizzling summer day, sandy beaches, coffee with friends, Thanksgiving dinner with family, and baseball games in June are all snapshots of heaven. Put all those amazing moments together and maybe you get a picture of what heaven will be like.

SNAPSHOTS OF HEAVEN

Kids have to be one of God's greatest glimpses of heaven. Jesus loved having kids around; He said they reminded Him of Heaven: "Let the children come to me. Don't stop them! For the Kingdom of Heaven belongs to those who are like these children."[6]

You see, kids have a perspective on life that adults lose. The true story is told of a third-grade girl who raised her hand when her teacher was teaching about whales and said, "I know of someone who was swallowed by a whale."

"Really?" the teacher responded with surprise. "Where did you hear that?"

"At church," the small girl answered. "My Sunday school teacher told us about Jonah in the Bible."

"Ah, I don't think you can believe that. You see, everything in the Bible isn't necessarily true."

"Okay," the girl answered right back. "Then I'll ask Jonah when I get to heaven."

"Well, what if he didn't make it to heaven, and he's in that other place that's not so good?" the teacher pressed. Without hesitation, the little girl snapped back, "Then you can ask him!"[7]

Yikes, don't mess with kids.

Something about the innocence, trust, joy, love, and passion of children made Jesus say, *Children are a snapshot of heaven.*[8]

Friends are another snapshot of heaven. As John continues with his description of heaven, he tells us, "The wall was made of jasper, and the city of pure gold.... The city walls were decorated with every kind of precious stone."[9] Some theologians are convinced this refers to the beauty of community in heaven—relational beauty. No more six-foot-high concrete-block walls will divide homes. No more broken marriages. No more abuse. No more split families. No more loneliness.

Isolation is for hell.

People sometimes say really foolish things like, "If all my friends are going to be in hell, I want to be there too!" Really? Like hell is happy hour? It's not. That's pure foolishness. It's not like that; aloneness is a snapshot of hell.

Hell is the ultimate loss of relationship and community. The most awful part of hell is the eternal separation from God and all people. In C. S. Lewis' *The Great Divorce,* the main character takes a bus ride through hell. The homes are far apart and dark, people are nowhere to be seen, and smoke is rising in the distance. He can't wait to get out of hell.[10]

But that's not heaven. Heaven is for friendships. Heaven is for love. Heaven is for singing with friends we love.

God loves music; that's why He put it on earth. And if God put music here, I'll guarantee you He's got more in heaven. That's why I tell people, **music** is a snapshot of heaven. Because isn't there something truly heavenly about slipping on your headphones in a noisy airport terminal and listening to Leeland, or Sanctus Real, or The Afters? And it doesn't have to be "Christian" music to be heavenly—I hear the beauty of heaven in songs like KT Tunstall's "Heal Over" or Jack Johnson's "Banana Pancakes."

And I'm not just making this stuff up. John, who saw heaven, said, "Each one had a harp.... And they sang a new song."[11] The crowds in heaven will sing. The angels sing. Music will fill the halls of heaven.

The writers of the Bible often used the imagery of **weddings** to describe heaven.

> As a bridegroom rejoices over his bride, so will your
> God rejoice over you.[12]

> The kingdom of heaven is like a king who prepared a
> wedding banquet for his son.[13]

> The wedding of the Lamb has come, and his bride
> has made herself ready.[14]

Weddings are a snapshot of heaven because something NEW is happening; someone pure is being welcomed; a promise is being kept; there's joy and dancing; two families are being made one; something very wonderful is in the making.

So every time you see a bride and groom kiss, God just showed you a bit of heaven

Coming **home** from a long trip always reminds me of heaven. When King David longed for home, he longed for heaven: "I will dwell in the house of the LORD forever."[15]

Home is where the Father is. We read in the Bible that our Father will be with us in heaven—"God himself will be with them."[16]

Jesus talked about our home in heaven. He once said, "In my Father's house are many rooms; if it were not so, I would have told you."[17]

Jesus was in construction, so He knew what He was talking about. When men from Arizona arrive in heaven, they're going to talk a lot about the houses Jesus built. I think the most stunning thing for them will be the fact that all the houses are not covered in stucco and painted beige.[18]

I'm convinced that when men from Arizona get to heaven, they will talk about stucco: "Look! God didn't just use stucco to side the houses in heaven! He used brick siding, wood siding, aluminum siding, vinyl siding. And look at all the colors He painted heaven—it looks like Puerto Rico!"

Jesus also said, "I am going there to prepare a place for you."[19] He really is. He loves you that much. I know you're not thrilled about leaving earth yet, but He can't wait for you to get to heaven.

It's kind of like the movie *The Notebook*. Allie and Noah are in love. And as they take a walk, she tells him of her dream house:

> "I want a white house with blue shutters and a room overlooking the river so I can paint."

> Noah replies, "Anything else?"

> "Yes," Allie continues. "I want a big ol' porch wrapped around the entire house where we can drink tea and watch the sun go down."

Noah's response to her is profoundly simple.

"Okay," he says.

Allie responds, "You promise?"

Noah replies, "I promise."[20]

Not long after this exchange, Allie chooses someone else she believes will make her happier over Noah. The man doesn't.

In spite of her absence, Noah builds her dream house ... and waits. He waits for the day she will come home and sit with him on the front porch of their big white house to watch the orange sun sink into the blue lake.

Jesus waits for you like that. He's preparing your home. He's a custom builder. Just as He designs every snowflake and fingerprint, He builds a life just for you—here and in heaven.

That's why going home is a lot like going to heaven.

Finish lines make me think about heaven. Paul, in the New Testament, was a runner. I believe that's why he loved runner analogies.

I press on toward the goal to win the prize for which
God has called me.[21]

I have finished the race, I have kept the faith. Now

there is in store for me the crown of righteousness,
which the Lord … will award to me on that day.[22]

This is the only race worth running. I've run hard
right to the finish, believed all the way.[23]

My good friend Tom was in town recently. He's a runner; actually he is a triathlete—he runs, bikes and swims.

While he was here, the annual Tempe Iron Man competition was going. So late Sunday night he talked me into driving to downtown Tempe to watch the last of the triathletes cross the finish line.

As we walked to the finish line after parking, we could hear from blocks away the announcer's voice boom over the PA system, "This is Jim Williams coming down the shoot. He's an engineer from Chandler. Jim. You—are—an—Iron Man!!"

I got chills.

Heaven's going to be like that. Luke writes, "That's the kind of party God's angels throw every time one lost soul turns to God."[24]

It got better.

At nine o'clock the music stopped as the announcer said, "The next three hours are very special. Because none of these athletes who cross now believed they would make it. They began this race seventeen hours ago and are barely hanging on."

"Around the world," the announcer continued, "at this special hour, the nine o'clock hour, we play this same song: 'Streets With No Name.'"

Just as he finished, a man came running down the chute. Tom leaned over and said, "He has one leg." But when I saw him running,

I couldn't believe it; he had no limp. His gait and stride were perfect. I had to stretch over the barrier to see that his other leg was replaced by a steel prosthetic. And it hit me—heaven will be like that. All the damage and loss will be gone, all the pain will be over, all the tears will be wiped away, and you will be whole again.

The Bible says, "All that's left now is the shouting—God's applause!"[25] The crowds, the angels, Jesus, and God Himself will stand there and cheer and shout your name ...

_____ _____, you did it!
You are a godly man [or woman]!
Welcome home!
Welcome home!

Hope that God Will Save the Day

Maybe that says it all. Our most final hope is that, in the end, God will save the day. He always does.

When we traveled to the Egyptian Sinai Peninsula to climb Mount Sinai, we spent our first night on the Red Sea. Wide-eyed from jet lag, I wandered out of our hotel at daybreak to sit on the shore. As the sun climbed over the horizon, I looked out over the deep blue waters toward the Egyptian mainland where the Israelites would have begun their crossing. It's a long way across a dark sea. I imagined how hopeless the children of God must have felt when they reached the banks. The Red Sea is blue, and vast, and deep. The dust of the Egyptian army was on their heels. But when life seems impossible, God is at His best. In a God-sized moment, He split the sea. The ground was dry. God saved the day.

When life is desperate and your heart floods with hopelessness, know that God will save the day. He restores what is lost and broken. He makes everything beautiful. He walks with you on life's dark nights. He fills your days with love and goodness and your soul with hope.

I know this because when Jesus Christ Himself was placed in a dark tomb on black Friday, God saved the day.

He showed up and put the sun in Sunday.

He

brought

daylight

to

a

dark

planet.

HOPE OF HEALING

Looks can be deceiving,
but I'll keep on believing,

in the faith higher above,

an unconditional love.

Not everything is true,

but I believe in you.

God the higher power,

save me in my darkest hour.

I look up for a sign,

to help me through this lonely time.

He reaches out his hands,

I know he understands.

He's teaching me a lesson.

so I can make progression.

He helps me get along,

so I can carry on.

With God nothing's impossible,

He brings all lives a meaning.

He makes you feel unstoppable,

and brings you hope of healing.[26]

Amanda Gott

NOTES

Foreword
1. Matthew 4:8–9 NASB.

Chapter 1: Darkness
1. Mark 14:32–50.
2. John 19:41.
3. Brennan Manning, *The Ragamuffin Gospel* (Sisters, OR: Multnomah, 2005).
4. Henri Nouwen, *The Wounded Healer* (New York: Image Books, 1990), 81–82.
5. Shusaku Endo, *Silence* (New York: Taplinger, 1969).
6. C. S. Lewis, *The Problem of Pain* (New York: Simon and Schuster, 1996).
7. E. A. Melville, "In the Night," AllPoetry.com. Used with permission.

Chapter 2: Boulevard of Broken Dreams
1. C. S. Lewis, *The Problem of Pain* (New York: Simon and Schuster, 1996), 86.
2. Isaiah 58:6–7, 10.
3. Darkys Black, "Fade," AllPoetry.com. Used with permission.

Chapter 3: Dark Night of the Soul

1. Richard Rohr, *Enneagram II* (New York: Crossroad, 1995), 14.

2. From Luke 18:9–14 (author's paraphrase).

3. Joshua 7:11–12 (author's paraphrase).

4. For more on the foolishness of sin, see Cornelius Plantinga, Jr., *Not the Way It's Supposed to Be* (Grand Rapids, MI: Eerdmans, 1995).

5. C. S. Lewis, *The Great Divorce* (New York: The MacMillan Company, 1946), 106–109.

6. Ephesians 6:12.

7. Luke 18:13.

8. Andy, "Sadness," AllPoetry.com. Unable to contact author.

Chapter 4: Silent Nights

1. Shusaku Endo, *Silence* (New York: Taplinger, 1969), 169–171 (author paraphrase).

2. Ibid., 168.

3. Ibid., 171.

4. C. S. Lewis, *The Problem of Pain*, (New York: Simon and Schuster, 1996), 23.

5. Alvin Plantinga, *God, Freedom, and Evil* (Grand Rapids, MI: Eerdmans, 1977), 30.

6. Richard Rohr, *Job and the Mystery of Suffering*. (New York: Crossroads Publishing, 1998), 45.

7. Ibid., 39.

8. Paul Brand and Philip Yancey, *Pain: The Gift Nobody Wants* (Grand Rapids, MI: Zondervan, 1993), 117.

9. Ibid., 121–122.

10. Philip Yancey, *Where is God When it Hurts?*, (Grand Rapids, MI: Zondervan, 1990), 268.

11. Ibid., 130.

12. 1 Kings 19:11–13.

13. Hebrews 13:5.

14. Hebrews 4:15.

15. Horatius Bonar, *Night of Weeping*, (Ross-shire, Great Britain: Christian Focus Publications, 1999), 144.

16. John Stott, *The Cross of Christ*, (Downers Grove, IL: InterVarsity Press, 1986), 329.

17. Yancey, *Where is God When It Hurts?*, 130.

18. Sabrina Correll, "On the Inside," AllPoetry.com. Used with permission.

Part II: Gray Days

1. ESV.

2. Matthew 27:63–64.

3. 1 Kings 19 (Mount Horeb is another name for Mount Sinai).

Chapter 5: Dirty Little Secrets

1. All quotes taken from PostSecret.com.

2. 2 Samuel 11:1.

3. 2 Samuel 11:2.

4. Dietrich Bonhoeffer, *Temptation* (New York: Simon and Schuster, 1959).

5. 2 Samuel 11:3 (NASB).

6. 2 Samuel 11:4.

7. 2 Samuel 11:5.

8. 2 Samuel 11:6.

9. 2 Samuel 12:7.

10. Psalm 139:1–3.

11. Psalm 51:2 (author paraphrase).

12. Anita Kelly, "Revealing Personal Secrets," *Current Directions in Psychological Science* 8 (1999): 105–109.

13. Psalm 51:7.

14. Frederick Buechner, *Wishful Thinking* (New York: HarperCollins, 1993), 18.

15. William Young (speech, The National Pastors Convention, San Diego, CA, February 2009).

16. Author unknown, "Through Shades of Gray," AllPoetry.com.

Chapter 6: Fear Locker

1. Brennan Manning, *The Ragamuffin Gospel* (Sisters, OR: Multnomah Publishers 2005), 148.

2. John Ortberg, *If You Want to Walk on Water, You've Got to Get Out of the Boat*, (Grand Rapids, MI: Zondervan, 2001), 118.

3. Steven Pressfield, *War of Art* (New York: Grand Central Publishing, 2003), 40.

4. Jeremiah 29:11.

5. John 14:16 (DBY).

6. Psalm 27:1.

7. Psalm 34:17–18.

8. C. Basham, "Watch the Angels Fly," AllPoetry.com. Unable to contact author.

Chapter 7: The War of Fog

1. Sherwood Lingenfelter and Marvin Mayers, *Ministering Cross-Culturally* (Grand Rapids, MI: Baker Books, 1986), 24-25.

2. From Luke 9:57–62.

3. Luke 10:40.

4. Luke 10:41–42.

5. Laura Shapiro, "The Myth of Quality Time," *Newsweek,* May 12, 1997.

6. Charles Swindoll, *Intimacy with the Almighty* (Nashville: Thomas Nelson, 2000).

7. Psalm 46:10.

8. Lowell Ganz and Babaloo Mandel, *City Slickers,* directed by Ron Underwood (1991; Los Angeles: Columbia Pictures, 2001), DVD.

9. Harley Brunswick, "Letter to My Father," AllPoetry.com. Used with permission.

Chapter 8: The Hand in Front of Your Face

1. NLT.

2. "Burundi: Albino Mother and Son Are Killed in Continuing Violence," *New York Times,* May 7, 2010.

3. Ibid.

4. Exodus 3:7–8.

5. Exodus 8:1.

6. Ecclesiastes 2:1–11.

7. Ecclesiastes 4:1.

8. Proverbs 24:11-12 (MSG).

9. Psalm 72:1 (author paraphrase).

10. Jason Ryan, "Justice Department Files Suit Against Philly Swim Club." ABC News, January 14, 2010, http://abcnews.go.com/Politics/justice-department-files-lawsuit-philly-swim-club/story?id=9557146 (accessed December 14, 2010).

11. Judges 21:25.

12. Isaiah 1:16–17.

13. Micah 6:8.

14. Luke 4:18–19.

15. Luke 10:25–37.

16. Katherine Dedyna, "Babies teach school kids to see through others' eyes," *The Vancouver Sun,* http://www.vancouversun.com/entertainment/television/Babies+teach+school+kids+through+others+eyes/1889856/story.html (accessed December 14, 2010).

17. Revelation 21:3–4.

18. Brian Misinale, "Beat," AllPoetry.com. Used with permission.

Chapter 9: You

1. Author paraphrase.

2. John 10: 3–4, 14.

3. From Mark 1:19–20.

4. From Luke 19:1–5.

5. From John 11:32–44.

6. From John 20:10–16.

7. From John 21:15–17.

8. "A Little Bit of Knowledge," *This American Life,* produced by Alex Blumberg, *NPR,* July 22, 2005.

9. Max Lucado, *Cure for the Common Life* (Nashville: W Publishing Group, 2005), 32-33.

10. Psalm 33:15 (NKJV).

11. Matthew 10:29–31 (MSG).

12. Jarrett Stevens, *The Deity Formerly Known as God*. (Grand Rapids, MI: Zondervan, 2006), 146.

13. Matthew 3:17.

14. Stevens, *The Deity Formerly Known as God*, 146.

15. From Song of Solomon 1:10.

16. Exodus 19:5.

17. Deuteronomy 14:2.

18. Isaiah 49:16 (NCV).

19. 1 John 3:1.

20. Chloe Sparacino, "Never Again," *Viewpoint* 22.2:11, Summer 2010. Used with permission.

Chapter 10: Mercy Drops

1. Gary Thomas, *Sacred Pathways* (Grand Rapids, MI: Zondervan, 2002), discussed in John Ortberg, *God Is Closer Than You Think* (Grand Rapids, MI: Zondervan, 2005), 121–134.

2. Luke 10:29–37 (NLT).

3. Lamentations 3:22–23 (ESV).

4. Psalm 111:4 (BBE).

5. Psalm 136 (NKJV).

6. Psalm 145:8 (KJV).

7. Ephesians 2:4.

8. Micah 6:6–7 (NLT).

9. Micah 6:8 (TNIV).

10. Fritz Kling, *The Meeting of the Waters* (Colorado Springs: David C Cook, 2010), 42.

11. Betty Klinck, "'Alternative' spring breakers steered from Haiti missions," *USA Today*, March 8, 2010.

12. *Anderson Cooper 360, CNN*, April 6, 2010.

13. Matthew 18:23–35.

14. 1 Samuel 24:1–7.

15. Psalm 23:6 (NKJV).

16. Author unknown, "God, Please Help Me," AllPoetry.com.

Part III: Bright Mornings

1. NKJV.

2. Psalm 23:4.

3. John 8:12.

4. Leonard Sweet, *Soul Salsa* (Grand Rapids, MI: Zondervan, 2000), 31.

5. Ibid.

6. ASV.

Chapter 11: Désolé

1. KJV.

2. Damaris P., "Sweet Sorrow," AllPoetry.com. Unable to contact author.

Chapter 12: Take Her Back

1. MSG.

2. C. S. Lewis, *The Problem of Pain,* (New York: Simon and Schuster, 1996), 103.

3. Anne Lamott, *Traveling Mercies* (New York: Anchor Books, 2001), 134.

4. Associated Press, "Stinky Christmas," MSNBC, December 26, 2007.

5. Psalm 88:6 (MSG).

6. C.A.M, "I'm Sorry," AllPoetry.com. Unable to contact author.

Chapter 13: Heal Over

1. Genesis 25:29–34, 27:1–41.

2. Psalm 137:7.

3. Obadiah 1:10.

4. Obadiah 1:4, 11.

5. Psalm 137:4.

6. 1 Corinthians 11:25 (author's paraphrase).

7. Callie Hansen (TheatreFreak), "Dear Storm," AllPoetry.com. Used with permission.

Chapter 14: Hold On

1. John 10:27–28.

2. Isaiah 41:10.

3. 1 Chronicles 4:10.

4. Psalm 139:10.

5. Job 2:9.

6. Author unknown, "Save Me, Please," AllPoetry.com.

Chapter 15: Daylight

1. This idea on hope comes from John Ortberg, *Living the God Life* (Grand Rapids, MI: Zondervan, 2004), 165–166.

2. Psalm 118:24.

3. James 1:27 (author paraphrase).

4. 2 Corinthians 1:3–4.

5. Psalm 23:6 (KJV).

6. Matthew 19:14 (NLT).

7. David Jeremiah, *25 Years of Laughter* © 2008 Turning Point.

8. From Matthew 19:14.

9. Revelation 21:18–19.

10. C. S. Lewis, *The Great Divorce* (New York: The MacMillan Company, 1946), 20–22.

11. Revelation 5:8–9.

12. Isaiah 62:5.

13. Matthew 22:2.

14. Revelation 19:7.

15. Psalm 23:6.

16. Revelation 21:3.

17. John 14:2.

18. This idea comes from John Ortberg, *Everybody's Normal Till You Get to Know Them* (Grand Rapids, MI: Zondervan, 2003), 256.

19. John 14:2.

20. *The Notebook,* directed by Nick Cassavetes (2004: New Line Home Video, 2005), DVD, quoted in Frank Viola, *From Here to Eternity* (Colorado Springs: David C Cook Publishers, 2009), 69–70.

21. Philippians 3:14.

22. 2 Timothy 4:7–8.

23. 2 Timothy 4:7 (MSG).

24. Luke 15:10 (MSG).

25. 2 Timothy 4:8 (MSG).

26. Amanda Gott, "Hope of Healing." AllPoety.com. Used with permission.

SCRIPTURE REFERENCES

Unless otherwise noted, all Scripture quotations are taken from The Holy Bible, New International Version®, NIV®. Copyright © 1973, 1978, 1984 by Biblica, Inc™. Used by permission of Zondervan. All rights reserved worldwide. www.zondervan.com.

Scripture quotations marked ESV are taken from *The Holy Bible, English Standard Version.* Copyright © 2000; 2001 by Crossway Bibles, a division of Good News Publishers. Used by permission. All rights reserved.

Scripture quotations marked NLT are taken from the New Living Translation of the Holy Bible. New Living Translation copyright © 1996, 2004 by Tyndale Charitable Trust. Used by permission of Tyndale House Publishers.

Scripture quotations marked NKJV are taken from the New King James Version. Copyright © 1982 by Thomas Nelson, Inc. Used by permission. All rights reserved.

Scripture quotations marked NCV are taken from the New Century Version. Copyright © 1987, 1988, 1991 by Word Publishing, a division of Thomas

DISCOVER MORE ONLINE:

www.GodCantSleep.com

or read more by Palmer Chinchen:
True Religion: Taking Pieces of Heaven to Places of Hell on Earth
www.TrueReligionBook.com

For more about Palmer Chinchen, visit
www.PalmerChinchen.com